This edition
is reserved for
Friends of History

LOST CIVILIZATIONS

HENRI-PAUL EYDOUX

FACTS AND ENIGMAS IN ARCHAEOLOGY

EDITIONS FERNI

French title:

Réalités et énigmes de l'archéologie

Translated by
Alex Scott-Kilvert
James J. Kigin

CONTENTS

foreword

The unravelling of the past, through the study of books, has practically exhausted its limits, and today archaeology assumes a vital role in the interpretation of history. This science demands a knowledge of many different fields, and employs difficult techniques. But it is generally rewarded by highly satisfying results. For several decades, it has been responsible for every major historical discovery, and has given us a clearer insight into past centuries and millennia which, until recently, appeared hopelessly obscure. Even when remains are dug up, which belong to a period already familiar to us, they still constitute an important contribution, by their concrete presence and by the truthfulness of the stories they tell. In short, archaeology has to offer a direct view into the past, which becomes almost tangibly alive.

In this book, I have attempted to record a few great archaeological discoveries, most of them recent. They have taken place in many different parts of the world, and have thrown light on a great variety of civilizations. My sole aim has been to demonstrate the decisive relationship between archaeology and history, by evoking random times and places of the past, which means that ancient France has been given but a minor importance in these pages.

H.-P. E.

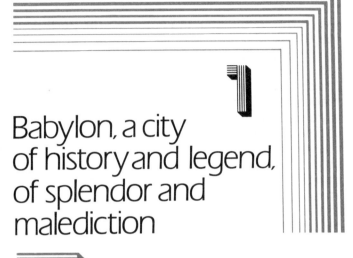

Babylon, a city of history and legend, of splendor and malediction

There exist a number of famous cities, whose very sites have been obliterated from the face of the earth. Such indeed is the case of Babylon, which calls to mind with melancholy Seneca's famous lines, "For all the cities which have, through the centuries, imposed their domination, for all the monuments which have adorned empires with their grandeur and their beauty, a day will come when, on the very places where they stood, one will wonder wherever they could be."

Few towns, however, have been so pregnant with history as Babylon. All the peoples of the East possessed it in turn: the Akkadians, the Kassites, the Hittites, the Elamites, the Assyrians, the Neo-Babylonians, the Persians, the Parthians, the Greek Macedonians, and others too. All the great conquerors left their mark there: Hammurabi, Sennacherib, Nebuchadnezzar, Cyrus the Great and Xerxes, Alexander the Great, who made it his Asian capital and died in it. The Jews were deported there, and, as if its history had not been enough, legend has been piled upon legend, one of the loveliest being that of Semiramis. It held one of the Seven Wonders of the World, the Hanging Gardens; and the Tower of Babel was built there to climb up to the sky. It was the object of the most dithyrambic praises as well as the most vehement denunciations ("the mother of harlots and of the abominations of the earth," in the Book of Revelations). Many times destroyed, it rose each time from its ashes reborn, the phoenix of cities.

Babylon is situated a little over sixty miles south of Bagdad on the banks of the Euphrates, which once flowed through it, assuring the region great fertility. It had too often filled the chronicle of history and the album of fair legends to become lost to the memory of men. Its vast ruins stood as impoverished witnesses to its past grandeur.

Exploring the site

The first man to give some precise information on the site was the rabbi, Benjamin of Tudele, in the twelfth century. A native of Tudela in Navarre, he traveled to visit Jewish communities as well as for reasons of commerce. "Babel," he notes, "is now entirely destroyed. There still remains Nebuchadnezzar's palace, inaccessible because of snakes and dragons."

It was only in the nineteenth century, when Mesopotamia began to allow access to travelers and archaeologists, that the exploration of the site of Babylon was undertaken. We owe the first research to a Frenchman, Fulgence Fresnel, who was assisted by a young German orientalist, Jules Oppert, and by the architect, Thomas. The French Government granted them a budget of 70,000 "francs-or"(1). In those days, archaeological expeditions were generously provided for. Fulgence Fresnel was the youngest brother of the famous physicist, Augustin Fresnel, the creator of crystalline optics; a member of the consular service, he had distinguished himself at an early age as an Arabic scholar. He could not withstand the Mesopotamian climate and the physical strain of the exploration. In 1855 he died in Bagdad. Mesopotamian archaeology had its pioneers, but also its victims. As for Oppert, he was a picturesque individual, and one of his biographers could not help saying of him, "you could have put him on stage to portray the popular idea of a scientist." He had a prodigious gift for languages and France, his country of adoption, was later to

1. Gold standard.

load him with the distinctions he deserved: a professorship at the "Collège de France", and a chair at the "Institut".

After this first campaign of exploration, Babylon fell back into obscurity. It was a German expedition which took up the work again in 1899. It was led by a great archaeologist, Robert Johann Koldewey. He was to uncover the legendary city in the reality of its town-walls and doors, its palaces and temples, its houses and streets. It is all the more to his credit since he found nothing but ruins. Generally speaking, one should not expect to find in Mesopotamia imposing ruins or dilapidated monuments, such as they come to light within the territories of Greece or the Roman Empire. The regions of the Tigris and the Euphrates are poor in stone; there dead towns usually have nothing to show but mere shapeless heaps and mounds of rubble.

If buildings had accumulated over the centuries, it was especially the most recent Babylon, that of Nebuchadnezzar, who reigned from 605 to 562 B.C., that the excavations unearthed. He was a giant among rulers, a warrior, the conqueror of Jerusalem, but above all one of the greatest builders of all time, as his rebuilding of Babylon bears witness, with its enormous chessboard layout, its huge edifices of temples and palaces.

The looting of Hammurabi's Code

At the time of the German excavations of Babylon, the French archaeologists were exploring the famous Iranian site of Susa. In 1901 they brought to light an object of capital importance to the history of the Near East, Hammurabi's Code. A great sovereign who, according to the latest archaeological data, reigned from 1792 to 1750 B.C., Hammurabi turned Babylon, up till then a somewhat unimportant town, into the capital of a unified and centralised empire, stretching from the mountains of Anatolia to the Persian Gulf.

The "Code" is an enormous block of basalt two yards high. It is crowned by a relief representing the king before Shamash, sun-god and god of ustice, who will dictate to him on the mountain a compilation of laws (surely this calls to mind Mofes receiving the Tables of the Law). Engraved in the form of a closely woven design upon the stone is the text of two hundred and eighty laws which a great orientalist, Father Scheil succeeded in deciphering in a few months.

Properly speaking, it is not a legal code, for Babylonia lived under a system of law dictated by usage, but rather a compilation of jurisprudence. Private and social life, administration and economy, find their place in this legislative monument.

This code, which is at the Louvre Museum, was not discovered at Sippar (close to Babylon), where it was erected, but a long way from that town, at Susa, as I have said. This find bears evidence of looting carried out on a large scale, and the lion of Babylon (which I shall discuss later on) is undoubtedly another proof.

In any case, this act of pillage was fortunate. A long time ago it probably saved from the destruction of Babylon this exceptional document which demonstrates the degree of civilization attained in Babylonia as far back as the beginning of the second millenium B.C.

The great temple and its "ziggurat"

There were a considerable number of temples in Babylon. The most important one was the Esagil, the temple to Marduk, the supreme god of the town. It was erected about nine hundred yards to the south of Nebuchadnezzar's palace. It would be useless to search for remains there; nothing much is left, for the Germans had to abandon extensive excavations. In fact, they found it under a layer of ruins over seventy feet thick, and they shifted 900,000 cubic feet of earth.

The archaeologists became laborers to discover it. They had to make the best of it by determining the contours and marking some key points. Imagine, then, the temple, comprising two juxtaposed wholes stretching for more than two hundred yards. The god sat on a throne and, according to Herodotus, the divine representation, made entirely of gold, weighed no less than eight hundred talents, which equals twenty tons of precious metal.

Near the temple rose the "ziggurat". This was a temple tower built close to the great Mesopotamian sanctuaries. There has been much debate as to its purpose, but today it is thought that it was a sort of majestical pedestal to enable the gods to descend to the level of men.

A ziggurat consisted of an enormous, solid mass, built on a rectangular base in successive stepped-back stages and equipped with ramps and staircases, varied in number from three to eight, according to the reconstructions which have been attempted. A chapel crowned the edifice. The main part of it was built of unbaked brick and the ornamentation of baked bricks held together with bitumen. We know of the existence of more than thirty ziggurats dispersed throughout the world: Assyria, Babylonia, southern Sumeria, as well as Elam in Iran, where the ziggurat of Tchoga Zanbil was unearthed by French archaeologists and is one of the best preserved.

The ziggurat, erected at Babylon near the Esagil, was enormous, even monstrous. We must take it to be the Tower of Babel. The famous passage in Genesis describes the descendants of Noah wishing to build a tower "whose top may reach unto heaven." But God destroyed their insane ambitions and punished their pride by throwing their language into confusion and dispersing them over the face of the earth. An excellent description in Genesis is worth quoting; it is of Mesopotamian structures. "Go to, let us make brick, and burn them throughly. And they had brick for stone, and slime had they for mortar." This method of building could not fail to amaze the Israelites, whose stone buildings in Palestine were held together by mortar.

In search of the Tower of Babel

The search for the Tower of Babel had been the constant aim of ancient travelers to Babylonia. Artists, on the other hand, could not wait. They portrayed it according to archaic representations. It appears even during the Romanesque period in the mural paintings of St. Savin, and later in the mosaics in the cathedral of Monreale in Sicily. Sculpture represents it in the Doge's Palace in Venice. It was a favorite theme for Brueghel the Elder, Raphael in the Loggias of the Vatican and many other painters. One could compile an endless iconographical list on the portrayal of this tower throughout the ages.

The Tower of Babel had been supposed at various times to exist either at Borsippa (today called Birs Nimrud), or at Aqarquf, about eighteen miles from Baghdad, where impressive remains of ziggurats still stand. This hesitation in locating the famous tower is understandable for the ziggurat of Babylon had been reduced to nothing and, mighty as it must have been, nothing visible remains.

In 1913, fourteen years after the start of work on the sight, the Germans began excavating. Despite the meticulousness of their research we would be very scantily informed about the famous monument if we could not refer to other facts. First of all, comparisons can be made with other cities, whose ziggurats have remained passably well preserved, for example those of Ur and of Tchoga Zanbil in Susiana. Then there is a short description by the Greek historian Herodotus, a great traveler and a faithful narrator. All that Herodotus saw of the tower were ruins, as it had been destroyed shortly before by the redoubtable Xerxes. Next, there is a very precious document, in the form of a clay tablet which can be seen in the department of Eastern Antiquities in the Louvre. It is modestly displayed in a corner of a glass case. Eight inches tall and less than four inches wide, it was found in a private collection by Father Vincent Scheil, the eminent orientalist, who translated Hammurabi's Code. The Louvre was able to acquire it. This tablet describes the Esagil and the E-Temen-an-Ki.

There is no doubt about the form of the base of the Tower of Babel. It was a square, measuring about 95 yards to a side. It is surprising indeed to ascertain the amount of agreement on this figure. Herodotus speaks of a stade, or 95 yards, and the Louvre tablet of a 180 cubits, which equal 93 yards. As for the German excavators, they arrived at the precise figure 94$^{1}/_{2}$ yards. Much can be said to the credit of these ancient surveyors.

On the other hand, we are less informed about the height of the tower. There is no reason to doubt the assertion of the tablet that the height was equal to one of the sides of the base. It was made up of several stories—seven, it is thought— so many cubes of decreasing volume placed on top of one another. The mass of the tower was built of unbaked bricks, but faced with an ornamentation of baked bricks. As to the stairs and ramp which led to it, their arrangement has caused much debate.

In any case, one can grasp the enormity of the monument, and how much it must have stirred the imaginations of men. It is difficult to realize the immense work required for its construction. According to an inscription, "all the peoples of numerous nations" were forced to work on it. The work was undertaken by Nabopolassar, who reigned from 625 to 605 B.C., by order of the gods who gave him, through the words of an oracle, all the necessary instructions. Nebuchadnezzar carried on the work and completed it.

This monument had only a relatively short life. At the most it was a century and a half, since Xerxes destroyed it. One of the first tasks of Alexander the Great, after entering Babylon, was to raise it up again and to return to Marduk, the god of the city, an abode worthy of his might. First the ruins had to be cleared away. This was an enormous task which, according

to Strabo, required 600,000 working days.
Koldewey found a veritable tell whose enormous mass consisted, he considered, of the rubble of the dead ziggurat. The death of the Macedonian conqueror had stopped the work and no one after him would have contemplated such a huge enterprise.

The Hanging Gardens

Enumerating the Seven Wonders of the World has beguiled many people, and the Hanging Gardens of Babylon are rarely omitted. In fact, its evocation stirs the imagination, and centers around the legend of the Queen Semiramis who is said to have built them. Yet, one wonders what the name means and how gardens can be considered to be hanging. Fortunately, ancient authors have written about them; Diodorus of Sicily, Strabo and Quintus Curtius. The ancient required descriptions of them in order to include them in this veritable contest of masterpieces which the Seven Wonders of the World constituted.

A tourist arriving at Babylon immediately investigates their location and wonders how long they flourished. A notice, driven into the ground on the left, before the Gate of Ishtar, reassures him: "Hanging Gardens." He is likely to be disappointed: lower down, he sees remains of enormous structures—not very engaging, perhaps. If he descends, he walks into a kind of labyrinth.

Vaulted rooms are set on either side of a central corridor inside a quadrangular enclosure.

These ruins, brought to light by German excavators, correspond quite well with the descriptions of ancient writers. They wrote thus of several vaulted, stepped terraces supported by great square pillars, rising one above the other until they reached the summit of the neighboring walls. On these terraces had been heaped layers of earth, so deep that huge trees grew there, "bearing as much fruit as if they grew on their natural soil."

"From afar," said the historian Quintus Curtius, "one imagines that one is looking at forests growing on the crest of mountains." It is known that this fantastic construction was at the highest point of the town. These gardens, of course, had to be much watered. "A column, hollow from top to bottom, contained hydraulic machines which hauled up great quantities of water, and none of this could be seen from the outside."

This hoisting machine supposedly consisted of an endless chain fitted with buckets which carried up the water, drawn from underground. Now German archaeologists have come across a triple well which could have provided this water. It is known, also, that the gardens were embodied in the great Palace which the Germans have named "Südburg", and which spreads its remains over an immense area: 310 yards by 200. All this suggests that Koldewey had indeed found the Hanging Gardens of Babylon.

A sumptuous Palace

To whom do we owe this Wonder of World? Today it is generally attributed to Nebuchadnezzar II, the great king of the neo-Babylonian dynasty. He reigned from 605 to 562 B.C. and restored to Babylon all its past splendor. A touching story exists that he had married a princess of Media, in the north-west of Iran. He wanted to offer his wife, summoned to live in the torrid plains of Mesopotamia, a setting of flowers and foliage to remind her of her native land, where the art of gardening was already highly developed.

After a sad glance at these poor remains of the Hanging Gardens, the tourist may well lose his way in the ruins of the great palace to which they were annexed. The dimensions, already given, were vast. The buildings were grouped around five big courtyards. The central courtyard gave onto the throne-room, which measures no less than 54 yards by 18, and at the end of it there is an alcove where supposedly the king sat. Standing among the ruins of this palace today, it is difficult to imagine its sumptuous effect and the splendor of its embellishment. It was the work of different kings of the neo-Babylonian dynasty, but especially of Nebuchadnezzar II. Fortunately, we have texts in which this famous king obligingly evaluates the importance of his work. These are grand pages for an anthology of opulence.

"I rebuilt the palace, my royal abode, a bond

between strong peoples, a house of joy and
happiness, in which I caused tributes to flow.
I laid its foundations with brick and bitumen on
the ancient foundations, reaching down as far
as the underworld. I had great cedars brought
from the Lebanon, a magnificent forest . . . In the
doorways I fitted cedarwood panels faced in
bronze—masterpieces in craftsmanship—and
thresholds and hinges. I heaped in the palace silver and gold, precious stones, everything of value
and beauty, riches and precious goods . . . .'' This
comes from "Babylone" by Marguerite Rutten.

This palace, brought to the height of luxury
by Nebuchadnezzar II, did not for long remain
the seat of the royal might of Babylon, for about
50 years later the Persians were to seize the town.
The Achaemenid kings kept up the famous palace,
and even built on to it. Its last guest was the
illustrious Alexander the Great. He took up
Nebuchadnezzar's words, "In my heart, I do not
desire my royal dwelling to be in another town . . .
In Babylon, there was no other place worthy of
my royal residence." And there he was to die
in 323 B.C.

Semiramis, "enchantress and king"

Semiramis has already been mentioned in connection with the Hanging Gardens, and legend has
made her one of the most famous women in
history. One could compile an enormous cata-

logue of works, literary or artistic, dedicated to
her. Probably the most recent is the "Air to Semiramis" of Valéry.

> *Rise, oh! Semiramis, mistress of soaring*
>   *[desires,*
> *Heartlessly searching for glory alone.*
> *Your imperial eye yearns for the great empire,*
> *Made joyous by the rule of your unyielding*
>   *[scepter.*

Before Valéry's poem, there's had been the
five acts of Voltaire's tragedy, and a great opera
by Rossini, set in Assyria. For common mortals,
the name of Semiramis conjures visions of fairy
palaces and garden scents.

Historians, however, referred to Herodotus,
the Father of History, who lived in the 5th century B.C., to another Greek, Diodorus of Sicily, a
contemporary of Augustus, and to Valerius Maximus, a Latin historian who lived at the time of
Tiberius. But none of them was able to gather
more than legends of the queen of Babylon, which
had been created centuries earlier.

Exquisite legends surround the birth of Semiramis, making her a queen of elegance and
beauty. She was born of the secret love between
a goddess of Ascalon, on the Mediterranean, and
a mere mortal. Doves fostered her miraculously,
and then shepherds tended her. An important
Assyrian official fell in love with her while
traveling in this distant region. Struck by her

beauty, he married her and brought her with him to Nineveh.

At this time, the king of Assyria was attempting to conquer the Bactrians and met with stout resistance. Semiramis was then urged by her husband to intervene. As the saying goes, "When the greatest of men fails, a woman may succeed." Dressed elegantly in male costume, she took charge of the matter and seized the city which the king had been unable to capture. This was unfortunate for her husband who would have been better off without his interference. The king of Assyria was filled with astonishment by the exploits and the beauty of this woman and he took her for himself, but shortly after died. Legend adds that Semiramis ascended the throne at 20 years of age, raised magnificent buildings, and founded the city of Babylon. She then set off to conquer Egypt, and lands as far distant as Ethiopia and even India.

Alexander the Great is said to have found this epitaph of the queen in Babylon. "Nature gave me a woman's body, but my deeds have equalled those of the most valiant of men. Before my time, no Assyrian had layed eyes on any of the seas. I have seen four which no one has ever approached. I have made rivers flow where I commanded. I built paved roads to cross over impassable rocks. With my chariots, I have cleared paths never before trodden even by wild beasts. In the midst of all these deeds, I have found time for my pleasures and my loves."

Historians have marvelled at the beauty of Semiramis. "She was so beautiful," said Valerius Maximus, "that one day, when a revolt had broken out in her capital and she happened to be washing, she only had to show herself half naked and with disheveled hair, and order was immediatly restored." As for Diodorus, he attested that, while at the height of her power, she had invented "a practical and at the same time elegant garment, in which she could take part in her normal everyday activities, as well as riding to battle on horseback."

An attempt had to be made, however, to reconcile this enchanting images with historical reality. Archaelogists, who so often tend to supplement the deficiencies of written records, intervened to throw a shaft of light on the golden penumbra surrounding this famous queen. The deciphering of cuneiform inscriptions revealed some facts, but unfortunately all too few. It was established that the name of Semiramis was the transcription into Greek of that of an Assyrian queen Sammu-Ramat, the wife of a king who reigned at the end of the 9th century B.C.

A thought now comes to mind : Sammu-Ramat lived in the 9th century. Now the origin of Babylon lies far back in the darkest, most remote reaches of time. How can the valiant achievement of the founding of Babylon then have been attributable to Semiramis? The fact is that the Greek and Latin historians took Semiramis and another queen, Naqi'a, to be one and the same person. The latter appears on a bronze plaque, perhaps the decoration of a throne, which is kept at the Louvre. She lived two centuries after Semiramis and rebuilt Babylon which had just been mercilessly razed to the ground. So she was taken to be a real founder of the city, whereas she was only its restorer.

The facts now become clear. Should we blame ancient historians who have brought about this confusion of identities? They were relating facts which had taken place long before. Faces, personalities and memories of Mesopotamian queens must have become curiously distorted and blurred when history consisted only of legends carried down orally. Indulgence is needed. It is only recently that we have been able to see clearly the dynasties and chronology of Mesopotamia. Herodotus or Diodorus of Sicily were in no better position to untangle such complicated strands.

The captivity of Babylon

In a previous paragraph, Nebuchadnezzar II, king of Babylon, was mentioned. He built the most sumptuous of palaces and gave the town all its splendor. This monarch spent a large part of his long reign, 605 to 562, fighting the Egyptian Pharaohs in order to dominate Syria and Palestine. The kingdom of Judaea belonged to the Egyptian coalition, and he besieged and captured Jerusalem and deported thousands of leading citizens. A second siege, a few years later, brought about the destruction of the town, and the mass deportation of the population. This is the famous "Captivity of Babylon" which began in 586 B.C. and did not end for nearly 50 years.

"By the rivers of Babylon,
there we sat down, yea, we wept,
when we remembered Zion."

(*Psalms* 137, 1)

Babylon then became bitterly cursed, since Nebuchadnezzar's capital was the cause of all the ills of Jerusalem and of the Jewish people.

"O daughter of Babylon, who art to be
[destroyed;
happy shall he be, that rewardeth thee
as thou hast served us.
Happy shall he be, that taketh and dasheth
thy little ones against the stones."

(*Ibid.,* 8, 9)

This last sentence alludes to the barbaric custom of crushing to death the little children of a sacked town. The Jews were not content with lamenting their fate. They dreamed of a divine justice, of the destruction of the offending city.

"I will make thee a burnt mountain
and they shall not take of thee

a stone for a corner, nor a stone for
[*foundations;*
but thou shalt be desolate for ever."
(*Jeremiah,* VI, 26, 26)

Nebuchadnezzar had his capital surrounded by massive ramparts, which are considered to have attained 98 feet in height. The place might have appeared impregnable. And yet in 539 Cyrus the Great, king of the Persians, seized it without striking a blow. Accounts differ as to how it was taken. The Greek authors maintain that Cyrus employed an extraordinary strategy, and that he diverted the course of the Euphrates so as to enter the town by the river bed. Treachery is also spoken of.

Be that as it may, the king of the Persians respected Babylon. Babylonia was reduced to the level of a satrapy. Still there were rumblings of revolt, which brought about the intervention of Cyrus's successors, first Darius, and later Xerxes. The latter king could hardly have been depended upon for leniency. Stopping awhile at Thermopylae in Attica, he devastated Attica and Boeotia, captured the Acropolis of Athens in 480 B.C. and burned the city. The following year he was to punish Babylon, destroying its temples and ramparts, and sacking it.

Babylon, the Asian capital
of Alexander the Great

Babylon rose up again from its ruins, but was to vegetate, a slumbering city, when Alexander undertook his campaigns. In 331 the Macedonian, after cutting off the Persian Empire by his conquest of the Mediterranean coast, put an end to Darius's resistance in a decisive battle at Arbela (Arbil) in northern Irak. In what is now Kurdish territory. The Persian king took refuge in the mountains. Instead of pursuing him to prevent him from re-forming an army, the Macedonian leader marched obliquely towards the south to go to Babylon. This shows that he was probably anxious to win this renowned city, and to make it a kind of monument to his glory, which would never grow dim. He prepared a mighty attack. For its position was strong, encircled by walls, protected, besides by the Euphrates and by all the canals which encompassed it. What is more, Darius had despatched there one of his right-hand men, the satrap of Mesopotamia, Mazaïos.

The reputation of the Macedonian was such that the town unexpectedly threw itself open before him, and gave him such a sumptuous welcome that one may wonder whether it was not, for the most part, prompted by real sincerity. After all, for the Babylonians, the Persians had been nothing but conquerors, whose yoke they ill endured; even if Cyrus had appeared in a favorable light, Darius and Xerxes had devastated their city, and wreaked destruction there. Proud of their celebrated past and of their tradition of civilization, they were more willing to incline towards Alexander, the propagator of an elevated culture. He also appeared as a liberator.

The conqueror's entry into Babylon was so dazzling that it must forever be an inspiration to imagery. He stood on his chariot, and his path was a carpet of crowns. Everywhere, priests, notables and inhabitants were thronging the way, bearing the richest of gifts. Poets, musicians and panegyrists were among their number. Alexander offered a solemn sacrifice to Marduk, the Babylonian god, and decided to rebuild the destroyed temples.

The ancient city was designated the capital of Asia. The Babylonians could not help being sensitive to this consecration which flattered their vanity, and also promised fruitful trade. No gesture could have been more favored by the population, so religiously fervent, so obedient to its priests, than the rebuilding of Marduk's temple and the great ziggurat, which the redoubtable Xerxes had destroyed.

Unfortunately, the work was so huge that it could not be completed. Strabo reports that 10,000 workers had to be employed for two months, as has been said, for the clearing away alone of the site. Where this colossal monument once stood there remains only a hole, filled with stagnant water.

Reliefs of fantastic animals on the gate of Ishtar, in Babylon.
Photograph by the author

The excavating of E-Sagil, the temple of Marduk, on the ancient site of Bab
One can appreciate how far below ground level this now is, in places as dee
75 ft. *Photograph by the author*

The death of the conqueror

In the spring of 323, Alexander returned to Babylon. Delegations came from all around to congratulate him and to request his alliance and his arbitration. He was truly set up as the monarch of the universe. Bad omens, however, had been occurring. Invoking bad auspices, priests had advised him not to enter the town, but he took no notice. Soon there was a new and sinister presage: an individual rushed towards the throne the sovereign had just left, and sat in it. All this could not fail to cause a sensation.

Nothing could stop Alexander in his ventures, and now he coveted Arabia. He needed a great fleet. He recruited sailors in Phoenicia which, famous for its shipbuilding, would send dismantled vessels as far as the Euphrates. Others would be built in Babylon itself. On the nearby river, a port was fitted out, capable of harboring 1000 vessels.

At the same time, Alexander mustered a new army. The greater part of it was composed of Persian recruits, 20,000 in number, representing some of the most warlike peoples. These soldiers, armed with bows and javelins, were flanked by heavily armed Macedonians who would always occupy the three first and the sixteenth of the sixteen ranks, making up each unit. The dedication gives place to great ceremonies, in which the conqueror appears crowned and wearing the royal purple. Soon there would be the funeral of

Hephaestion. Alexander had regarded this Macedonian general as a brother, and had made him
the second most important person in the empire.

Hephaestion, guard of honor, had played a
decisive part in the battle of Arbela, which
marked the final defeat of the Persians. He had
died the previous year at Ekbatana, and his body
had been brought back to Babylon. Alexander
had sent his ambassadors to the oasis of Ammon
to consult the oracle of Jupiter about the last
tribute he should pay his best friend. The verdict
was late in coming: Hephaestion was not to be
honored as a god, but as a hero. In any case, he
was to have a royal funeral. His body was burned
on an enormous storeyed funeral pyre, like a
ziggurat, weighted down with magnificent ornamentation. After this 10,000 bulls were sacrificed
and a great banquet took place.

In actual fact, Hephaestion did not meet a
hero's end. He died of intemperance. This was
a bad example. After the funeral ceremony in his
honor, there were banquets for the next few days
ending late at night. During one of them, Alexander was taken with a violent bout of fever.

The outcome of his illness has been carried
down to us in detail in the reports set down, which
the Greek historian Arrien reproduced in his "Ana-
basis". The fever rapidly got worse, and Alexander, although growing weaker and weaker, gave
the order for the embarcation of the troops,
anticipating his own departure. He died on the
eighth day.

Of course, his death took on the proportions of a catastrophe, and gave rise to the most varied of rumors. Poisoning was suggested, names were quoted, and it caused a great stir. But such hypotheses are unnecessary. The Macedonian conqueror was prematurely worn out by physical strain and by the excesses of all kinds in which he had indulged. In addition to that, there were the wounds he had suffered.

There is no doubt that conditions in Mesopotamia were unhygienic, and that it was devastated by malaria. Alexander failed to withstand the bout of fever which had struck him down. When he died in 323 B.C., he was 32 years and 8 months old. It is sometimes said that his work remained incomplete. Of course, he could have added to his conquests and drawn into his orbit other parts of Asia, notably Arabia, and overcome Carthage as well—granted that he had designs on the Punic capital. At least, he died gloriously in this illustrious town which he had wished to make his capital and whose reputation was commensurate with his genius.

The last days of Babylon

The death of Alexander the Great was to bring about that of Babylon. It seems that the famous city was unable to outlive him. A few years later, one of Alexander's generals, Seleucus I, Nicator, "the victor," subdued the Asian part of the

Macedonian empire, and founded the dynasty of
the Seleucids which was to rule for three centuries. It was not his intention to make Babylon his
capital. He founded a new capital after his own
name, Seleucia, about 40 miles from the old one.

But gods die hard, and during the Seleucid era
more temples were restored in Babylon. Afterwards, a Parthian king gave a final blow to the
town, destroying and burning the monuments,
and deporting the population. According to the
Greek geographer, Strabo, in the first century
Babylon was virtually uninhabitable. Here one
remembers the "Lamentations of Jeremiah".

> "... therefore the wild beasts of the desert
> with the wild beasts of the islands shall dwell
> there and the owls shall dwell there in
> and it shall be no more inhabited for ever
> neither shall it be dwelt in from generation
> [to generation!"
> "... it shall not be inhabited but it shall be
> wholly desolate everyone that goeth
> by Babylon shall be astonished and hiss
> at all her plagues."

Today the traveler visits Babylon at the risk
of being a little disappointed. The illustrious city
is no longer anything but an enormous expanse of
ruins. The Gate of Ishtar is the best preserved
whole structure. Herodotus spoke of a hundred
gates, but excavations have enabled us to ac-
knowledge the existence of only seven.

This gate, consecrated to the "Mistress of Battle" who was at the same time "Mistress of Love", measures 95 feet wide and 160 feet thick. Deprived of its top, only its walls and vertical supports remain. The latter, however, are decorated with a host of animals in baked clay—dragons, bulls and lions—which animate the dead architecture in a singular way. Nearly 700 were counted, standing out in light hues against a bluish background. A small part still remains in place, while a certain number of them have gone to the big museums.

Beyond the Gate of Ishtar, began the processional route which was 24 yards wide and 310 yards long. On either side rose a high wall adorned with a series of lions, the royal beast of Ishtar. There were 60 on each side, but nothing is left of them except a few lions lost in distant museums. One can wander on this road, hastily retraced several yards above the ancient level, where neither reason nor the imagination are easily satisfied.

At the end of this portion of road looms the "lion of Babylon" mounted on a miserable concrete base; but it is an extraordinary work. Of great dimensions—over 3 yards long—it represents a wild beast trampling on a fallen man, who is struggling. Carved in a basalt block, the coarseness of which hardly permitted refinement of sculpture, it appears to be merely rough-hewn. But in spite of that, what an impression of movement it conveys! The artist knew how to impart to his work an unequalled force, by the simplest of means, and by the adroit resolution of the bigger features.

Many hypotheses have been advanced on the origin, meaning and date of this work. It is thought that it could be Anatolian, and that it is booty of the Babylonian conquerors. Amongst many ruins, anywhere, few can convey such an oppressive sense of mortality than those of Babylon. The great events which took place there convey an overwhelming contrast. The might and glory that was has given way to the poverty following the downfall and destruction of the city. The fantastic history of this city calls for more substance to uphold and exalt it.

THE PRINCIPAL EVENTS OF
THE HISTORY OF BABYLON

−24th century	First mention of Babylon, believed to have been founded by the Akkadians.
−19th century	Foundation of the first dynasty of Babylon.
−1792 to **−1750 approx.**	Reign of Hammurabi, the first famous king of this dynasty.
−16th century	The Kassites, come from the mountains of the north-east, put an end to this dynasty. They held Babylon until the 12 th century.
−1550 approx.	Hittite raids on Babylon.
−1170 approx.	Raiding by the Elamites, who seized Hammurabi's code.
−12th to **−7th century**	Assyrian rule with periods of independence.
−689	Sennacherib, the king of Assyria ravaged the city.
−680 approx.	His son Asarhaddon rebuilt it.
−625 to −605	Reign of Nabopolassar, the founder of the neo-Babylonian dynasty, and the builder of the Tower of Babel. Allied to the Medes, he destroyed Nineveh in 612. End of the Assyrian Empire.
−605 to −562	Reign of Nebuchadnezzar II the great king of the neo-Babylonian dynasty. Conqueror of Jerusalem. Restored Babylon to its former splendor.
−586	Deportation of the Jews to Babylon.
−555 to −539	Reign of Nabonide(s), last king of the neo-Babylonian dynasty.
−539	Cyrus the Great seized Babylon, which was allied to the Persian empire. He assumed the title of "king of Babylon."

−480 approx.	Xerxes in suppression of an usurper pillaged the town and deported its inhabitants.
−331	Alexander the Great entered Babylon and made it the capital of his Asian empire.
−323	Alexander the Great died there.
1852	First "scientific" exploration, carried out by the Frenchmen Fulgence Fresnel and Jules Oppert.
1899-1917	German excavations led by Robert Koldewey.

(The sign − indicates B.C.)

A strange deposit of masterpieces under a street of Piraeus

It happened in Piraeus on Saturday, July 18, 1959. In this summer month when the sun blazes and Greece is oppressively heated, laborers had begun work at day-break. Two of them, Andreas Sakellion and Nikolaos Kordonoris, were working not far from the harbor, on the south side of George I Street, at its intersection with Philon Street. Leaning with all their strength on pneumatic drills, they were breaking up the road for a company commissioned to build a sewer.

Passers by quickened their pace to avoid the dust that was being thrown up and the throbbing noise of drills. Suddenly all was silent. Andreas Sakellion and Nikolaos Kordonoris had stopped working and were bending over the ground.

Chance, the archaeologist's salvation

A bronze hand had appeared in a clod of earth. The workers immediately informed their foreman, Hippocratis Terzis, who in turn called two employees of the company, who gave the order to stop digging and to alert archaeological authorities. These were the first witnesses to a sensational discovery, due to chance, as in so many archaeological finds. Magnificent masterpieces of Greek art had been lying for centuries not so very deep under the street.

The crowd was now gathering. In a town so crowded and so teeming with life as Piraeus, news travels fast. A hand dug up from the ground was certainly a small matter, but could not be expected to be the only one. What are called salvaging operations had to be begun at once. The workers became assistants of the Archaeological Department. The sewer could wait. The hour had struck for the exploration of the past.

The heat had become overwhelming, but that was of no importance. It was necessary to take one's time, and everyone set to work with the slow minuteness and respect required for the unearthing of history. Soon two bronze arms appeared. It became clear very quickly that they belonged to a male statue, a "kouros" the forehead embellished with curls, in an obviously archaic style. At his side, came to light a young girl of striking beauty, whose feet lay next to the head of the kouros. A "cippus", with Hermes's face engraved on it lay above the latter, while on top of the female statue were fragments of a metal shield.

The crowd grew bigger. Several thousand people were packed together in Philon and George I streets, when, at 5.0 p.m., it was decided to halt excavations and to transport these first findings to the Archaeological Museum of Piraeus. The caretaker, Dimitri Kaladonis, suffered an arm injury during the loading. The truck cut a difficult path through the enormous mob, which immediately re-formed, in front of the Museum. That evening, members of the government came to pay homage to the two bronze statues which, on that happy day of July 18, had unexpectedly enriched the heritage of Greece.

Excavations were carried on during the following days with the same gathering of people. They were led by Mr. Janni Papadimitriou, Director of Attic Antiquities. He was unfortunately to die in the beginning of 1963. On July 25, exactly a week after the first discovery, another surprise lay in store. In a trench for excavation, there appeared folds of clothing of a bronze statue lying on its back. The more the workers got it out of the earth, the more they were struck by the vastness of its dimensions; they found themselves confronted by a giant statue. One can understand the agitation the archaeologists felt in seeing, little by little, a truly colossal work, seemingly in perfect condition take shape in the dry and dusty earth, that hot summer's day.

While the excavators made slow progress, in spite of their impatience, measuring every move and taking infinite precautions, they discussed the matter at hand. For a while they were led onto a false track. That is, another smaller bronze statue appeared to the right of the big one, and was turned towards it, apparently embracing it. There was thought to be a group of them. Work continued to free it. In fact, the statues turned out to be two separate works brought together by chance: a helmeted Athena, measuring 9 feet 5 inches, and an Artemis, half as tall. The bronze of the latter was corroded, and its arms, with which it embraced Athena, were broken during the excavation. Luckily it would not be difficult to restore them.

What an extraordinary apparition these two goddesses were, closely reunited by fate in this corner of Attica which had become a stretch of road! The goddess of war and the goddess of hunting lay together: she who protected Ulysses at all times, and she who was forever fierce and untameable. Fate had willed that they, who were so different by nature in the celestial pantheon, should lie side by side, because of haphazard acts of men, for two millennia.

But the fruits of that eighth day of excavation did not stop there. A piece of marble appeared near Athena's head. It was the shoulder of a female statue, the only one not in bronze. When it was brought to light, the experts could not decide what it represented and, as will be shown later on, it is still a mystery. The collection was completed by the discovery of a great mask of tragedy in bronze, and a second cippus with Hermes' head, even finer than the one which had been found on the first day of excavation.

Treasures buried under a few inches of soil

Those few days had reaped an extraordinary harvest, but the excavations had to stop there. The street was soon to take on its usual appearance, and there was nothing to show the impatient motorist that a precious deposit had been hidden for two millennia under a few square yards of road.

It is incredible to think that the statues had remained buried almost at ground level, some only 3 feet under the modern highway, and the deepest at 5 feet. It needed little, during the centuries, for some random pick-axe to come and wake them from their sleep. Moreover, it was a fortunate coincidence that in this part of Piraeus a street should pass over the site, on which a house could just as easily have stood. Perhaps the bronzes, which would have been dug up during the laying of the foundations, would then have been dispersed, or quite simply been carried off by thieves. The chronicle of archaeology is thus filled with treasures lying almost at ground level. There is one at Vix, which was brought to light in 1953.

But the archaeologists' work did not merely consist of digging up the precious material. They took infinite care in studying how it all had come to be placed in this manner such a long time ago. In this way, they found that the statues had been carefully stored—side by side, or one on top of the other—in a room with flimsy walls and whose foundations, about 2 feet deep, have been cleared on two sides. This room measured about 6 yards in length. Similar structures had been found in 1956, when work was being carried out near a small neighboring church.

There is no doubt that these were shops or storage rooms situated near the harbor. The magnificent bronzes had been stacked there with a view to their being shipped. They were covered with a thick layer of ashes and of fragments of roofing-tiles. An arm of the kouros had been blackened by fire. Therefore a dramatic event had occurred when the statues were to be loaded, and the remains of the burnt-out building had buried them—nearly—forever. This affair dates back to the 1st century B.C., as has been proved by the discovery of a coin. Later on, interesting hypotheses which have been advanced on this subject will be discussed.

The remarkable kouros of the archaic period

The kouros is probably the most important work to be yielded up by the soil of Piraeus. Its beauty is astonishing and, in addition, it has the privilege of being the most ancient bronze statue of great dimensions—6 feet 5 inches tall—to have come down to us. It is thought to belong to the 6th century B.C. Some even suggest a more specific date of origin—530-520 B.C.

This is the middle of the archaic period of Greek art. A formal study of Greek art and history is not intended here. However, a few reminders seem necessary. The archaic period begins after Homer, at the beginning of the 8th century B.C., and end with the Medic wars, which began in 490 and so cruelly struck Greece. This was an extraordinary era of blossoming art. Greek architecture in stone is foremost with its classic orders; sculpture was rapidly attaining perfection with original creations.

Here are seen to emerge these two very characteristic types of human portrayal: the "kore" and the "kouros". The first is a clothed young girl, generally holding an offering in her hand. We know of excellent examples kept in the Museum of the Acropolis. The Kouros is a young man, shown nude, with the right leg forward. For a long time, it was believed that he represented Apollo, but today this interpretation has been abandoned. The kouros and the kore are undoubtedly portrayals of votaries, which the Greek artists idealized as images of youth and beauty.

Let us consider the kouros of Piraeus. It really is a masterpiece of archaic art. Nothing could be more perfect than this body which, although

frozen in a conventional posture, is alive with
movement. It personifies simultaneously strength
and grace. Behind the realism one can discern
an extraordinary vision of inner life, revealed by
a face on which joy and bliss are manifest.

Of course, one would like to know the name of
the artist who executed this masterpiece. Unfortunately, all one can say is that the statue probably
came from a workshop in the north-east of the
Peloponnesos. No more will ever be known. We
should be content to possess this relic enveloped
in all its mystery. Moreover, archaic sculpture has
remained implacably anonymous. We can barely
quote two names of sculptors of this period, and
we still know virtually nothing about them.

True, Greek art was to make up for this later on
with a whole catalogue of fashionable artists of
universal reputation: Phidias, Praxiteles and
many more.

Athena, the patroness of cities

The biggest object from the excavation of
Piraeus is the helmeted Athena, which measures
no less than 9 feet 5 inches. It is a magnificent work
of the 5th or 4th centuries B.C. One has the impression that the findings would have been incomplete
if they had not included this goddess, to whom
Athens is said to owe its name, and who was the
patroness of cities, assuring their survival. She
rose out of the soil of Piraeus as a symbolic appa-

"The Lion of Babylon", the famous Hittite sculpture, probably a booty of Nebuchad-nezzar II. *Photograph by the author*

Detail from a mosaic of Alexander the Great at the battle of Issos, in Cilicia. Mus of Naples. *Anderson-Giraudon*

rition, the protectress of citizens, and the symbol or reason and intelligence. The ravages of war were past and she reappeared in her peaceful serenity full of majesty. Her lips are delicately parted, as if about to speak. Her eyes, in onyx, are extraordinarily alive—the "goddess with the sea-green eyes."

This preference—this weakness almost—of Greek artists for the inlay of enamel, glass and precious stones was made possible by techniques of working in bronze. Of course, it is tempting to have reservations about such artifice, but they applied it brilliantly to give intense life to their work, and to confer on it a sometimes startling realism, which neither distorted nor degraded the objects they sought to idealize. One has only to consider the famous charioteer of Delphi. His eyes are of white enamel and of onyx, and his eyelashes of finely worked metal. The methods used are beyond criticism. He stares straight before him, but he seems to be lost in the distance. A radiant face shines intensely forth, one of the most handsome and engaging that art has ever produced.

Known representations and mysterious statues

The kouros and the Athena are the two most important works of the deposit from Piraeus, but we should not, on that account, neglect the other

statues. One of them remains something of an
enigma. It is the bronze statue discovered on the
first day at the same time as the kouros. Six feet
five and a half inches tall, it portrays a young girl of
great beauty. But who was she? She bears no
definite attribute. Some took her to be Artemis on
account of her belt and shoulder strap. Others,
such as Janni Papadimitriou, supposed her to be
Melpomene, the goddess of tragedy, and this
hypothesis seems more likely. She might be
compared with the great bronze mask of tragedy,
18 inches wide, which the excavations yielded.
The muse could well have held it in her outstretched right arm—but she would have had
great difficulty in carrying this very heavy mask. It
is more likely that this object decorated a theater of
Athens or Piraeus.

On the other hand, the Artemis, found on the
8th day of excavations and at the same time as the
Athena is perfectly characterized. It is a very fine
work, belonging to the 4th century B.C., 5 feet
2 inches tall, and it really does portray a classic
image of this goddess, who took pleasure only in
hunting and who used her bow as much on human
beings as on deer.

There is only one marble statue in the whole
collection. It is 3 feet 6 inches tall and in perfect
condition and, like the young girl in bronze found
at the same time as the kouros, it is impossible to
say what it represents. It is clad in a long tunic
which touches the ground and touches the feet,
and, above, a veil frames a face full of sweetness

and grace, covering the folded arms and reaching to the knees. It is impossible to say whether this is a goddess or a priestess. One is inclined to take it for a votary of some Eastern religion.

This collection, dug up from the soil of Piraeus, is most strange and disparate. There are bronzes and marbles, the statue of a man, and several of women—goddesses and others without identity—shields and a mask of tragedy. Whoever raided the place made no mistakes. He took only sculptures of major importance. For him, the subject or material of a work were unimportant. He greedily collected odds and ends, which he considered to be beautiful, and, in order to hasten and facilitate the removal, he took the statues without their pedestals. A collector would have been concerned with unity and chosen works which were roughly similar to one another.

In this instance, everything seems to point to an act of pillage, as will be described further on. The statues were gathered together hastily without any preconceived choice. Probably they were taken from various temples and buildings, which were unscrupulously plundered. The scene is easy to imagine, with arguments about the masterpieces, and the dismantling and the careless loading onto carts, which were promptly despatched to the harbor. It is not known how many loads were thus made up. Some were shipped away by departing vessels. Others remained stored in the docks.

A dramatic atmosphere

As described above, a coin was found with these statues. This is the only clue to a date of burial. The coin bore inscriptions of Athena, helmeted, and Zeus surrounded by lightning, as well as a symbol—a star between two half-moons which was soon identified as being that of Mithridates the Great. Even the date the coin was put into circulation was specified: 87-86 B.C.

This was a dark page in Greek history. For sixty years, the country had been under Roman rule. It was the end of the independence which, despite a bitter rivalry between cities, had blossomed into civilization and beauty. The Greeks rebelled briefly and were treated severely by their new masters.

A Hellenized barbarian, Mithridates the Great, the king of Pontus—the very one whose coin was unearthed in Piraeus—had roused Asia against Rome, declaring himself to be its "most mortal ennemy." He had massacred all the Italians living there, 80,000 of them, the historians assure us. Soon Delos, then Athens, fell into his hands.

Greece was on the verge of freeing itself from Roman rule. But Sylla acted in time. He was a cold-blooded man, who would not hesitate to carry off a "coup d'Etat" to save his position of command. He undertook the Eastern campaign. In 87, he besieged Athens and Piraeus, which resisted till the spring of the following year. The Acropolis held out for several months more. In 85, he signed a peace treaty with Mithridates on the basis of the "status quo" before the war. Sylla was lenient, because Rome was in the throes of civil war, and he was anxious to have a free rein in Greece and in the East.

It is not intended to enumerate here, even briefly, all the episodes of such a violently coloured history, concerning which there is an abundance of literature. The taking of Athens by Sylla could be likened to a horror story, and Plutarch, who wrote about a century later, has left us this account of it. The Roman soldiers breached the walls and the dictator "entered Athens in the middle of the night, in terrifying apparel, to the sound of bugles and trumpets and the furious cries of all the army. He had authorized the soldiers to loot and murder, and they swarmed into the streets of the town, wielding swords, and performed the most horrible acts of carnage."

The historian adds, "the number of those massacred has never been known. Even today, one can only judge by the places that were covered with blood... Several actually maintain that it flowed out of doorways and trickled as far as the outskirts of the town." But the tyrant Aristion had taken refuge in the Acropolis, and there he held out, before finally being forced to give up the struggle, overcome with thirst. Shortly afterwards, Sylla took possession of Piraeus and committed acts of great destruction there, "in particular" Plutarch specified, "that of the arsenal built by the architect Philon, which was a marvellous work."

Could these buried remains come from Sylla's pillaging?

The evidence is categorical: Sylla's campaign was marked throughout by the imposition of tributes and by pillage. The dictator made the Greeks pay dearly for their rebellion and their loomed at all times the cheerless shadow of the 80,000 Italians massacred in Asia. What is more, the campaign was expensive, and Rome then in the midst of civil war, could hardly be depended on to send funds. Also, the troops looked more like a rabble than an army, and it was wise to keep them well rewarded, in order to ensure a loyalty of sorts.

So Sylla felt no respect for even the treasures of the temples, which were held to be sacred. Epidaurus, Olympia and Delphi were despoiled. "In order to win over to his side the soldiers of an enemy" Plutarch goes on to say, "he (Sylla) lavished on his own men endless gifts and favors. Therefore, he needed vast resources to buy the treachery of some, and to provide for the intemperance of others." Nothing was spared. In Piraeus, Sylla took for himself a rich library, which held most of the works of Aristotle and Theophrastus, "which were not yet very widely known of," and had them taken to Rome.

As we can see, everything seems to indicate that the magnificent remains, found on the July 18, 1959, were part of the Roman booty. The statues would have been stacked in a shop in the harbor, ready to be shipped. What happened then? Sylla must have returned to Italy, which he is to reconquer with the same cold cruelty he showed when he overcame Greece. So he had other things to do than to complete this vast removal of works of art and treasures which he had begun. Should one believe that this wealth was so abundant that some of it could be left behind? The objects in gold and silver must have had priority over the humble bronzes and marbles which could be scorned. Or else the burning of the shop, where they were stored, quite simply buried them under the ruins, veiling them for centuries.

Of course, the evocation of Sylla's appalling war and of the ensuing acts of pillage fall like a shadow on this discovery in Piraeus. The little coin of Mithridates the Great, found with the statues, is a compelling reminder. But all this is mere hypothesis, and one must be cautious in reconstructing history.

The touching signature of Phidias at Olympia

I t is rare for an artist to earn universal and unanimous approbation. Phidias enjoyed such a privilege, and the recognition of his genius, praised by his contemporaries, grew with the passing centuries. His name alone symbolizes the perfection of Greek art, and he is considered by all to be the greatest sculptor of antiquity.

In fact, we know little about him, and if one applies known facts, his biography is soon written. His date of birth is agreed to be around 490 B.C. He probably died in 431, reaching a considerable age for the time. His talent would perhaps have remained unknown, if a prime opportunity to express it had not been presented to him by

Pericles, an Athenian statesman to whom the "golden century", the most enlightened era of ancient Greece, owes its name.

It was Pericles, then, who entrusted him with the supervision of a building-site without comparison. He wanted to make an impressive statement of the triumph of Athenian democracy and to embellish the city, by endowing it with an imposing monument, the Parthenon, sanctuary of Athena Parthenos. A woman played a decisive role in affording Phidias with protection and unreserved friendship: Aspasia, Pericles' lover, who has been qualified as an "enigmatic and seductive muse." She was, in reality, a courtesan. But this term should not be understood in the pejorative sense. One is more inclined to think of a "geisha" of antiquity, combining beauty with intelligence and wit.

Aspasia came from Milet, on the coast of Asia Minor, and was, therefore, a foreigner to Athens—which cost her not a little hostility. She was a schemer, but a most cultivated one. Socrates enjoyed her company, treating her on equal terms, and it has even been related that he was passionately in love with her. She held a literary and artistic salon of sorts, and this perhaps explains why Mme de Staël was to admire her so deeply. It was a remarkable salon, frequented not only by Socrates, but also Euripides and, of course, Phidias. And Plato would in turn pay his respects to the famous courtesan in one of his "Dialogues". Even if, in a jocular vein, he jeers at the Athenians who used funeral orations as a pretext to do excessive praise to the living, he assures us that Aspasia excelled in this "genre".

In Pericles' time, the Greek city was exclusively in the hands of men. One can imagine how the intrusion of a woman like Aspasia must have appeared scandalous in this wholly male society. Those who were uncompromising considered that Pericles owed everything to Athens, that he was the soldier-citizen whom nothing should distract from his task, above all not a woman. The polemicists mercilessly gave forth; Aspasia was called a courtesan, a lustful woman; they called her Juno or the modern Omphale. The two lovers stood up to these outbursts of public opinion.

Aspasia played an important part in the great Athenian revolution of the 5th century, during the famous "golden century". When one wanders around the Acropolis, it is difficult not to imagine her ghost roaming amongst the dead colonnades. And when one speaks of Phidias, it is fitting to do homage to the woman who provided him with such a deep friendship.

A statue in gold and ivory

It is difficult to say exactly what part Phidias had in the architecture and the furnishing of sculptures in the Parthenon. In any case, he inspired and arranged all of it. Of course, by its very size, the work had to be collective, but there is

no doubt that Phidias directed operations from
beginning to end. The unity of conception and of
execution confirms this. The monument bears
throughout the stamp of the master.

As well as sculpture, Phidias practised all arts:
architecture, painting, even jewelry. His genius
was to arouse much jealousy and, because of his
close ties with Pericles and Aspasia, people
sought intercourse with them through him. He
is said to have met a wretched death. There are
somewhat contradictory accounts on this. One
tradition has it that he misappropriated considerable sums of the consecrated treasure of Athens.
According to another version, a cabal was set
up, accusing him of embezzling ivory; this cost
him a prison sentence, during the course of which
he died, or so it is said.

The prevailing belief is that he took refuge at
Olympia, where he sculpted the famous statue of
Olympian Zeus. Phidias gained much glory by this
statue and by that of Athena Parthenos, and the
latter sat enthroned in the Parthenon. Both have
disappeared, but ancient writers who were
dazzled by them left accurate descriptions. Five
centuries later, the Stoic philosopher, Epictetus,
was not afraid to write, "Go to Olympia to behold
Phidias' work. It would be unfortunate to die
without having seen it."

These two giant statues were "chryselephantine". This seems a curious term. It is composed
of two Greek words: "Khrusos" meaning "gold",
and "Elephas" meaning "ivory". Works of art

were often made of ivory and gold together. The Greek artists excelled in this technique, but probably Phidias was the only one to use it for statues of huge dimensions.

When one reads in Pausanias, the Greek geographer and historian, the description of Phidias' Zeus, one feels a certain embarrassment. Granted, he achieved perfection in his style. But the means he used offend our present-day taste for simplicity and for the attainment of beauty without excessive artifice. The god was represented sitting, holding a scepter in his left hand and a victory in his right. He was over twelve yards in height and Strabo recorded, "if the god were to stand up, his head would go through the celling." The unclothed part of his body—torso, head and arms—were in ivory. The clothing and the throne were in gold, inlaid with ivory, ebony and precious stones.

We should note that neither the ivory nor the gold was solid, but merely a veneer. There was in all this a disconcerting display of wealth and a pursuit of gaudiness. But can we judge a work fairly by our current standards? Nothing was too lavish for the portrayal of Zeus, the greatest god of Greece, who commanded light and lightning, the king of gods and of men, enthroned on Mount Olympus. It must be remembered, as the leading historian of Greek art, Jean Charbonneaux, has pointed out, "that the Zeus of Olympia was a statue to be worshipped, that is, a venerated idol, through which the divine presence was revealed. More than any other statue, the idol had to look like a living being. It was looked after as carefully as a human person, and offered as many luxuries as a royal one.''

Thus is explained, and justified, that which might offend us in the very conception of the work, and in this combination of gold and ivory—the latter better able to render the visible parts of the body, giving them the appearance of living flesh, with the help of a little tinting.

In any case, the statue aroused mystical rapture in those who came near it. It was related that, on its completion, Phidias prayed to Zeus to let him know by a sign whether he approved of his work, and that, at that very instant, lightning struck the paving-stones in front of the statue as a sign of divine consent.

The resurrection of a site

Until the beginning of the last century, the famous site of Olympia had remained obliterated. Men and nature had combined in erasing it. It was built in the heart of a pleasant landscape at the foot of Mount Kronion, and next to two streams, the Kladeos and the Alphea, and their alluvia, as well as the erosion of the hills, had progressively covered up the ruins and formed a layer several yards deep. A hundred and fifty years ago, travelers who roamed about on the site of Olympia still saw no trace. Where was the colossal temple of Zeus, which had sheltered Phidias' chryselephantine statue? And the stadium, and the sporting-installations which witnessed, every four years, the famous Olympian games? And all the monuments which were clustered about the site? The travelers had to be content, under the shade of the fine trees growing in the valley, with reading Pausanias and the ancient writers who had enjoyed relating minute details.

The famous sanctuary had not, however, disappeared violently, as if Zeus, god of lightning, had mercilessly struck it down. It perished gradually. Sylla had plundered it, of course, as well as so many other places in Greece, but the Romans, always obsessed with Hellenism, had added many monuments. Until the end of the 4th century A.D. the Games took place there regularly, until prevailing Christianity put an end to them. The emperor Theodorus ordered the temples to be systematically dismantled, though he took care to have Phidias' famous statue of Zeus transported to Constantinople. But the god did not survive. His colossal image perished in a fire fifty years after his removal. Later, earthquakes finished off the remaining ruins.

France undertook the first excavations of Olympia, in 1829. The Greek war of independence was in full swing, and, ardently backed by public opinion, Charles X had sent an expeditionary corps. The Bourbon king was imitating Bonaparte's grandiose idea of the Egyptian campaign: to the troops, commanded by General Maison, he joined a team of engineers, scientists and artists.

This was modest in comparison with the Commis-
sion of Egypt, which included more scientists than
generals, but the team carried out good work.
The archeological part fell to Abel Blouet, then
aged 34, who was to distinguish himself later on in
restoring the public baths of Caracalla in Rome,
and in completing the "Arc de Triomphe" at
the "Etoile".

Blouet came to the site and saw only a few
scattered stones. He excavated steadily for six
weeks only, but he was fortunate. He had tackled
the great temple of Zeus, and came up with the
main dimensions and some important sculptures
which were sent to the Louvre. The Greek cabinet
authorized the French to take away the "bas-
reliefs", which were shipped by the vessel, aptly
named "Alphea". A few years later, Abel Blouet
published an important work which is still a useful
book of reference, "Scientific expedition to
Morea."

France had a special claim to the further exploration of Olympia, but curiously enough she lost
interest in this site, leaving the work to the Germans, who concluded in 1875 a formal treaty to
this end with the Greek Government. The first excavation campaign, which turned out to be singularly
fruitful, was provided by the "Reichstag" with a
considerable budget. Wilhelm Dörpfeld, who had
already won fame at Troy, was assigned to lead it.

Research at Olympia was taken up again in
1936, and the same year the Olympic Games were
held in Berlin. This was a perfect opportunity for

the German archaeologists to call attention to the site where these games had been born. They succeeded in making their point. New excavating-campaigns were launched, though interrupted by the war. Today, Olympia has been revived in its entirety, and it is one of the greatest triumphs of archaeology.

Inscribed on the base of a drinking-cup

In the heart of Olympia stood the temple of Zeus, where the sovereign god dwelt. There remains an enormous base, and sections of columns are lying all around. Even though sur-rounded by the poetry of the ruins, it is a melan-choly sight when one imagines what the vastness and the beauty of the sanctuary must have been. In the center, stood the giant statue whose pedestal bore the inscription, "Phidias, the Athe-nian, made me."

One problem for the excavators was the location of Phidias' workshop. The colossal nature of the work, the different materials of which it was composed, all the sculptured décor which went with it, required a large building. Until recently, there was hesitation between two buildings: one traditionally called "Phidias' workshop," inside which a Byzantine church was built later on, and another one adjacent to its south side. The German archaeologists have settled the question once and for all. They proved that the south building had been built subsequently, and what is more, they discovered, in the one thought to be the workshop, vestiges confirming its purpose, notably the remains of a bronze foundry. Nearby, they found considerable garbage dumps, where the artists threw away the waste matter from their work: moulds of the god's cloak and of clothes, bits of ivory, scraps of metal—iron, bronze and lead—semi-precious stones bearing saw marks.

All these findings displayed the whole range of all the different types of craftsmanship, which contributed to Phidias' work of art. What is more, they provided a decisive solution to a question of endless archaeological debate: of Phidias' two giant statues in gold and ivory, the Athena of the Parthenon and the Zeus of Olympia, which one was made first? The date of the former has been determined: it was completed in 438 B.C. There is uncertainty as to the latter. Now the many ceramics found in the Olympian workshop can definitely be placed around 430-420. There seems to be no more doubt that the priority falls to the Athena of the Parthenon.

The specialist, who was entrusted with the mass of potsherds collected during the excavation, patiently cleaned and restored them. One day, he discerned a small pot—a very simple drinking-vessel—which had been found in 1958. On its base, he perceived a graffito of several letters in classical handwriting. The reading was easy, "I belong to Phidias."

This was a startling and moving discovery. The famous artist had engraved these words. One can imagine him continuously working in his shop. The foundry is nearby and it is hot in the shop under the Olympian sun. Phidias is surrounded by his specialists and assistants. They drink frequently. The drinking-vessels are easily confused, and the master wants to have its own. So he engraves his name on it. This unhoped for discovery bore Phidias' signature.

Another discovery, also in 1958, caused a sensation. It was a bronze helmet of Corinthian design, and bore a name, Miltiades. The German specialists consider, for various reasons, that it belonged to the famous Athenian general, the conqueror of the Persians at Marathon. We can well believe that he made an offering of his helmet at the Olympian sanctuary. Today, in Christian pilgrimages, one can see military badges and decorations given by their owners. An exciting sense of history emanates from these findings of Olympia.

The long history of the Olympian games

Those who visit the site are overwhelmed by the immense work achieved by the archaeologists. The earth, which covered the ruins like a shroud, represented hundreds of thousands of tons. The most recent excavations came upon the stadium, which has been cleverly reconstructed, and today we can easily imagine there the gripping spectacle of the Games.

On vast slopes surrounding the stadium itself, the spectators—they could have been as many as twenty thousand—massed together, forming groups according to cities of origin, as eagerly do supporters at football matches of today. This was a solely male public, for in pursuance of a strict regulation, women were not permitted to enter the enclosure of the sanctuary or to be present at the sporting events. One single exception was made in favor of a priestess of Demeter. Distinguished guests, magistrates and priests sat at the tribune situated in the center of the southern slope, the foundations of which have been found by the excavators.

To the sound of trumpets, the members of the jury and the athletes came into the stadium by a narrow passage, and this lent a theatrical effect to their entrance. Then lots were drawn: the competitors each took a chip from an urn. All along the track, agents were positioned, equipped with whips and cudgels, to make sure that the rules were observed fairly. Besides, the behavior of the athletes had already been watched at leisure, for they had been at Olympia for several months, training under the guidance of their coaches.

Despite the solemnly sworn oaths, despite the threats that weighed upon them (if a rule was broken, their families, even their cities of birth could be held strongly responsible), there must have been some athletes who cheated. An ancient writer, Lucian, stigmatized them in biting terms, "The bad athlete, unable to win the prize and despairing of winning it by his speed, resorts to dishonest actions. He is bent on stopping, hindering or tripping up his opponents, convinced that victory will never be his, unless he acts in this way."

All these events took place in this stadium except, of course, the chariot races, which were held at the nearby hippodrome. They varied between thirteen and fifteen in number, and included running, a race in combat dress, flat-hand wrestling, boxing, pancratium (similar to a all-in wrestling), the throwing of the discus and javelin, jumping, and all the rest.

In 393 A.D. the Olympian games, which had been held 292 times, took place for the last time. The discovery of the site and the archaeologists' reconstruction of it have had much to do with the initiative taken by Pierre de Coubertin, who is justly commemorated by a monument built at the entrance to Olympia.

Cleopatra's beauty : legend and fact

n ancient historian said of her that she was so beautiful that a number of men were willing to give up their lives for a night with her. Another recorded, "She is wonderful to look at and to hear, and she captivated the souls of those who were the least amenable to love, even hearts that had been chilled by age."

The reader can guess straight away the name of this woman: Cleopatra.

Her beauty has been the subject of much discourse. Everything combined to promote it to the highest degree. This is not surprising. She had subjugated Caesar, the conqueror, and Antony, who was likened to Hercules. Only Augustus

resisted her charms; he was a little sickly,
it is true. For the sake of Rome's pride, such a
woman, capable of bending the will of the greatest
of Romans, had to possess exceptional beauty
and charms, and embody the characteristics of
an enchantress.

A faceless beauty

Subsequently, many things have been conducive to maintaining this reputation: artists,
poets and, even today, film directors. Not to
mention the scholars themselves who, so often
obedient to a cold severity, show some pleasure
in treating a personage such as Cleopatra. Here
they give way to a lyricism which treats with ease a
strict truth. In this connection, the English historian, Arthur Weigall, looks at Cleopatra as a
pleasant combination of the "femme fatale", and
of the "coquette", young and impulsive. Many
films have been made about her, and rightly so.
The question is whether the illustrious and last
queen of Egypt was in truth really beautiful. One
may well say: if we cannot trust the accounts of
historians, let us then turn to the work of artists.
But it is around that very subject that the serious
debate revolves: while so many empresses,
queens, the great and not so great ladies of
antiquity, have left us their effigies, we have no
real portrait of Cleopatra. There exists just one
sculpture—we shall see it later on, and it can be

considered with some certainty to represent her. This is thanks to the recent scientific study of a great specialist.

This artistic blank is so exasperating that there has been increasing attempts to identify Cleopatra in many anonymous busts. It is not intended here to make a list of these works. The principal ones are a "more than suspect" bust in the British Museum, and a head in the Museum of the Vatican, inadvertently placed on a body that does not belong to her, and it is agreed no longer to consider it a portrait of Cleopatra.

There remain coins, by which we have definite effigies. We are concerned mainly with a drachma minted in Alexandria, a tetradrachma of Ascalon, and tetradrachmae put into circulation at Antioch in 36 B.C. on the occasion of the marriage of Antony and Cleopatra. For lack of anything better, this series of coins is a precious source of informations, even if on the whole unsatisfying, and a well-known numismatist, Jean Babelon, stated with chagrin, "One of the most amazing personages in history has left but feeble traces for numismatics."

An enlightened sovereign, Juba II, king of Mauritania

Let us now move on to the Algerian coast. 62 miles west of Algiers stands the little town of Cherchell, pleasantly situated by the sea, in Louis

Bertrand's words, "of a nobility and grace remi-
niscent of Campania." Its featureless modern
houses, its peaceful little harbor, its quiet existence, certainly show no trace of the splendor it
knew in antiquity. What is more, there is no longer
any great monument. Rebellions, invasions,
earthquakes too, all left their mark in turn, leaving
only wreckage: demolished buildings and, now
arranged in a museum, numerous sculptures,
some of which are masterpieces, such as the
famous Apollo of Cherchell, found by chance
in 1910.

Cherchell served at first as a trading-post for
the Phoenicians, and was named after one of their
gods: Iol. After the ruin of Carthage, it fell under
Moorish rule. Subsequently, Rome applied in-
direct administration there, in order to economize
on funds and troops, and made it the capital of an
indigenous kingdom, setting over it a North
African, Juba II, who was loyal to Rome. This
kingdom, called Mauritania, was vast and
stretched from the region of Constantine in the
east to the Atlantic in the west.

Juba was a curious and, on the whole, a very
attractive personality. His father, Juba I, king of
eastern Numidia had, like so many others, taken
sides with Pompey against Caesar. He was to
regret this, for he was defeated and killed himself,
and his son, only five years old, was taken to Rome
and displayed in honor of the dictator's triumph.
This was indeed a brilliant and skilful political
strategy on the part of the Romans. Everything

was maneuvered for him to become a loyal and ardent Roman. He was raised in Caesar's family and especially by Octavia, Augustus' sister, who was considered the most accomplished woman of her time. When he was only just adolescent he was granted the freedom of the city of Rome. He was hardly to fail to become a zealous and almost blind servant of Rome, which was to set him on the throne of Mauritania, the size of which has already been stressed and which was cut out for his measure.

It is difficult to say whether Juba II was a great king exercising authority, whether he proved himself a good administrator. In any case, Rome pulled all the strings of African politics. He turned out to be what we call an enlightened sovereign. He left behind him in particular the memory of his culture, his leaning for the arts and for all knowledge of the intellect. He had unlimited pretentions in this matter, and wrote on many subjects. Even if we have nothing of him, we know in any case that many ancient writers plagiarized him, even Pliny the Elder, and Plutarch. Of his capital, called "Caesarea" in honor of the emperor, he made a city of pomp and fine monuments, where sculpture abounded.

Cleopatra Selene, daughter of Cleopatra the Great

Five years after his accession to the throne, Juba II married Cleopatra Selene, the very daughter of Cleopatra the Great and of the famous triumvir, Antony. This was a curious destiny. The unlucky girl whose parents were defeated at Actium and committed suicide, was taken to Italy and brought up at court, like her future husband, Juba II with whom she spent her childhood. Likewise, this prodigious woman, Octavia, Octavius' elder sister, played a part in her education. Ironically, Octavia was the wife of the triumvir Anthony, who repudiated her for Cleopatra the Great. There she was, in the name of sacrosanct Roman principles, bringing up the child born of her husband's treachery! Thus Rome summoned to reign over a large part of Africa two young sovereigns, whose parents had been desperate enemies of the Roman empire and had disappeared tragically from the public scene.

There is a bust in the Museum of Cherchell—it is reproduced in this book—of Cleopatra Selene, which was found in the town. The hair-style is very elegant. The hair, encircled by the royal diadem, is arranged in symmetrical wavy curls, while a fringe finely frizzed, adorns the forehead and the temples. Such a style is clearly Egyptian, and may be found in other effigies of queens of this Lagid dynasty, to which Cleopatra Selene belonged. The eyes are big and beautiful; the face

MONARCHS OF EGYPT AND
OF MAURITANIA

PTOLEMY XIII AULETES

Father of Cleopatra the Great. Ruled from −80 to −51.
Representative of the Greek Ptolemaic dynasty, founded
in Egypt in 323 by Ptolemy Soter, an officer of Alexander
the Great, also called the Lagid dynasty.

CLEOPATRA VII
(CLEOPATRA THE GREAT)

Last queen of Egypt. Born in −69. Ruled from −51 to
−30. She had a daughter by Mark Antony: Cleopatra
Selene (see below). After the battle of Actium, she committed suicide, at the same time as the triumvir. Egypt
was annexed to Rome.

CLEOPATRA SELENE

Daughter of Antony and Cleopatra. Raised at Rome.
in −20, married Jubal II (see below). Gave birth to
Ptolemy (see below). Died in −5.

JUBA II

Son of Juba I, king of Numidia, defeated by Caesar in
−46. Taken to Rome, at the age of five or six, appeared
in Caesar's triumph and was raised at the court. In −25,
he was placed on the throne of the kingdom of Mauritania, the capital of which was at Caesarea (Cherchell).
Ruled for nearly half a century, until +23.

PTOLEMY

Son of the above mentioned. Last king of Mauritania. Put
to death by Caligula in +40, in Lyon. Mauritania, now
permanently annexed to Rome, was divided up into
Tingitanian Mauritania (Morocco) and Caesarian Mauritania (Caesarea-Cherchell).

$$\left(\begin{array}{l} - : \text{B.C.} \\ + : \text{A.D.} \end{array} \right)$$

is full with rounded features, but a certain
hardness of expression and a sullen manner are
discernible, accentuated by the prominence of the
lower lip. Should we, for all that, subscribe to the
judgment of Stephane Gsell who wrote "This face
is masculine, if anything . . . We are in the presence of a virago . . . This Cleopatra certainly has
not inherited the bewitching charm of her mother"? This a severe and, no doubt, unjust appraisal.
To begin with, in this portrait, the queen is no
longer in the prime of life. Also the nose and chin
have unfortunately been chipped and this mars
the final effect of the work.

Juba, thanks to the clemency of Rome, returned to the land of his ancestors. There he was
able, in the course of time, to foster a civilization
of refinement. Cleopatra Selene, on the other
hand, was never again to see her native country.
She was always to feel a nostalgic attachment to
Egypt. One can imagine the sovereign, Romanized
as she was, in her heart—and publicly when she
was able—extolling her attachment to the famous
dynasty of the Lagides and venerating the memory of her mother, the last queen of Egypt of
tragic destiny. How could she fail to feel this grief
for her family?

When she bore a son, she named him Ptolemy,
wishing to recall her Egyptian ancestors. Unhappy
Ptolemy, the last to bear that name! The sinister
Caligula, jealous of him and of his wealth,
cowardly had him put to death in 40 A.D. in Lyon,
where he had invited him.

Reflections of royal Egypt are mirrored in Cherchell

Archaeological findings have confirmed this attachment to Egypt. Religious symbols and sacred animals of the valley of the Nile can be seen on the coins. Buried in a pit, there has been found a large and beautiful statue of Isis, the Egyptian goddess, wife of Osiris and mother of the sun-god. She was honored in Caesarea as far back as Juba's time: a sanctuary was built in her honor, and the king put there a crocodile.

Two other findings, also in Cherchell, are even more eloquent. Unfortunately, one of them has lost his head, and of the other only the lower part of the body remains. The first portrays a high priest of Memphis, who died aged 60, a contemporary of Cleopatra. The other represents a king of the 18th dynasty, Thoutmosis I, who ruled in the 17th century B.C. What are these two heavy statues, imported from the banks of the Nile, doing in Cherchell? It would seem obvious that Cleopatra Selene, a daughter of Egypt, wanted to have near her works of art to remind her of her country.

Everything seems to show that Juba II's wife was faithful to her native land and to her family ties. Rome nurtured her in its breast, and made of her a Latin princess. She was in no way rebellious and, like her husband, was a docile instrument of Roman politics. But in her heart, she felt a secret debt towards Egypt.

What is more, the king must have encouraged this attitude in her. He himself, although the son of a Numidian king, felt himself to be a native. He could not claim such a glorious lineage as that of his wife. Jérôme Carcopino has shown that he sought to fabricate a curiously implausible divine genealogy. He was a megalomaniac, all the more so in that his power, which he owed to the will of Rome, was insignificant. Thanks to his wife, he was to reflect a semblance of Egyptian royalty, and, a lover of culture, to remain, above all, prepossessed with that fair land of civilization and the arts.

An anonymous head

Let us now enter the museum of Cherchell. It was built at the beginning of the century, a vast courtyard surrounded by galleries. It is one of those museums which fill one with pleasure and, at the same time, confusion. In spite of the splendid objects it holds, practically nothing remains intact. They give the impression of having been systematically battered and broken. There is an impression of sadness, of fallen and destroyed beauty. That is all that remains of the collection of the king Juba who wished to embellish his capital with masterpieces. He has been compared to a tasteless millionnaire building up a museum, and, in addition, there were all the sculptures which high officials and

Like an exhumed corpse, the kouros lies resting after its discovery, in a room in the Museum of Piraeus. *Photograph by Megalokonomou*

One of the statues, discovered at Piraeus, of Athena.
Photograph by Boudot-Lemotte

rich inhabitants of Caesarea had later accumulated during the Roman period proper of the town.

Confronted by these poor relics, one can hardly imagine what must have been the accumulation of art treasures at Cherchell two millennia ago. They were dispersed until a recent date. When a European colony settled at the site of Caesarea at the beginning of the conquest, ancient stones were much used in building the modern city and a number of marbles were sent to the oven to be reduced to chalk. Because of this, the famous Venus of Cherchell nearly perished, so near to the Venus of the Capitol and the Venus de Medici, which is now in the Stéphane Gsell Museum in Algiers. An officer noticed it being wheeled to the oven by a worker, but for a piece of silver he made sure that the goddess changed directions.

But enough of these regrets, and instead of being carried away in the Museum of Cherchell it is sufficient to linger in front of a very big marble head—16 inches high. This is a beautiful face encircled by a veil. It was discovered on the property of Saïd, on the road to Algiers, and taken to the museum by Victor Waille, a professor at the Literary College of Algiers, who had led the excavations of ancient Caesarea since 1886.

This head has intrigued many archaeologists. It is probably a portrait, for the features are very personalized and the artist probably did not wish to idealize them. One may well wonder whom it portrays. Stéphane Gsell, a member of the Institute and chief inspector of Algerian antiquities and museums, gave this very uncertain description:

"Head covered by a veil. The ears are pierced as for ear-rings. It is, therefore, a woman, although many Numidian and Moorish men wore ear-rings (but this veiled head definitely looks Roman), even if the face has a masculine quality: prominently arched eyebrows, aquiline nose, a severe mouth, a haughty and imperious expression. This portrait, which certainly dates back to the first century A.D., we take to have represented Agrippina, Nero's mother."

One can see how this great specialist hesitated between the portrait being that of a man or a woman. In the end, he decided that it was a woman's effigy. He wanted to identify it and hypothesized Agrippina the Younger, then abandoned the idea.

The mystery is solved by a specialist

Thus the problem remained unsolved. It was agreed, however, to reject Agrippina the Younger as a candidate, for the head of Cherchell was much too estranged from what we know today, thanks to a very far-reaching study of Roman iconography. Who could it be then? In 1953, Jean Charbonneaux, director of antiquities at the Louvre Museum, happened to visit Cherchell.

This specialist was struck by the aura of mystery which surrounded the head of Cherchell and wanted to try to resolve it. He built up hypotheses, deductions and comparisons. He refused to accept the hypothesis of Agrippina the Younger, but in doing so, he did not want to replace it with that of Agrippina the Elder; yet the "imperious eminence" of the person portrayed could not be overlooked. Now, we are at Caesarea, the Mauritanian capital, the residence of Juba whose wife, as mentioned earlier, is Cleopatra Selene the daughter of Cleopatra the Great.

The research of Jean Charbonneaux naturally points to the illustrious and last queen of Egypt. This is a hypothesis which serves as a starting-point in the attempt to pinpoint the truth of the matter. One must not be carried away by all the arguments so far developed, but stop to enumerate only a few of them. The hair-style is clearly of Egyptian type. The queens of the Lagid dynasty, which had reigned over the banks of the Nile since Alexander's death, were portrayed veiled on most coins. The very style of the sculpture places it at the beginning of Augustus' reign. First and foremost, a definite point of reference must be found in the coin effigies of Cleopatra, interesting specimens of which have been discovered, as has been said earlier. But one is obliged at this stage to quote Jean Charbonneaux.

"The comparison of these profiles on coins with that of the veiled head seems to be conclusive, especially if we bear in mind the obvious attempt at idealization in the marble of Cherchell. The mouth is unfortunately damaged, but fate willed that the nose should remain almost intact, lacking merely its tip which points towards the chin; this disfiguration hardly sufficed to change the course of history. The comparison would be more conclusive if the hair were more in evidence, for the little we see of it corresponds satisfactorily with what the effigies on coins tell us . . .. They show that, in growing older, Cleopatra had increased the amount of coils in her hair . . .. The sculptor has brilliantly interpreted this coquetry of her hair when she was approaching forty.''

What date should we give the head of Cherchell? Jean Charbonneaux reckons that it is a posthumous portrait executed between 20 B.C., when Cleopatra was married and settled in Mauritania (her mother had died ten years before), and 5 B.C., when she died.

Thus Cleopatra Selene is said to have wanted to have the image of her famous mother near her. She was by no means ignorant of her life, her excesses and her mistakes too, but the pride she held in her ancestry and her tenderness towards her mother overruled these feelings.

Was the last queen of Egypt really beautiful?

The Cherchell bust, emerging thus out of a gloomy obscurity, has conveyed to us, in all probability, the image of this astonishing woman, Cleopatra, who was one of the most extraordinary figures of history. If one lingers over the statue, one finds oneself scrutinizing the features of the face and its expression, searching for the soul behind the marble.

Was she beautiful? The answer is no, if we consult the classical canons. Let us consider rather the somewhat crude facial structure, the aquiline nose with the pronounced tip and wide nostrils, the prominent jaw and lower lip. But in contrast, this bright face with big eyes emanates something a little haughty perhaps, but in any case an attractive and arresting manner of true majesty. We would do well, however, to avoid the worthless portrayals in which history and literature have indulged, such as these lines of José Maria de Heredia,

> *"Raising her pale face within dark hair,*
> *She tendered her mouth and clear eyes."*

Much has been said of her nose and her breast, allegedly bitten by the deadly asp, and a whole physiognomy has been built up, in the same way paleontologists reconstruct a mammal from a single bone or tooth. But have we read closely enough the ancient writers? First and foremost is Plutarch, a passage of whom deserves to be quoted here.

"It is claimed that her beauty in itself was not so incomparable as to enrapture with wonder and admiration. But intercourse with her had an appeal impossible to resist. The attractiveness of her face, sustained by the charm of her conversation and by all the graces which can enhance a happy nature, stuck deep in the soul like a thorn."

One need not read between the lines. Plutarch's appraisal is quite clear. He speaks of the "attractiveness" of her face, but recognizes that it was by no means marked by exceptional beauty. To what, then, was due her lure, her seductive power, which for a while compromised Rome? In particular, she had a "voice full of sweetness" and, "like an instrument with several strings", she spoke many languages; she possessed a refined intelligence, a wealth of culture and a lively repartee. She easily conquered Mark Antony, who had wanted to dazzle her and soon had to admit defeat, for "his jokes were, if anything, common and smacked of the soldier." She had a taste for display and a sense of stage-craft. There are famous passages depicting her, magnicently adorned, surrounded by a swarm of splendid women, sailing in a golden-pooped-barge, to the sound of flutes, lyres and pipes, among the scent of many perfumes which wafted to the banks of the river.

There is no lack of brilliant spectacles, and fanciful stories have been embroidered. Cleopatra has been endowed with exotic beauty, because it was forgotten that she was a Hellenized Macedonian. She has been depicted as a licentious woman, luring as many men as possible into her bed. One admittedly feels a certain discomfort in thinking that she was 22 when she gave herself to Caesar who was 53, ugly in appearance and bearing.

But it is this very affair with Caesar which enlightens us about Cleopatra's amorous activities. Showing how she trapped Mark Antony in her net, Plutarch writes, "She founded her greatest hopes on herself and on the magic of her charms." She hoped to protect Egypt's independence and to keep herself on the throne. Rome is a dangerous threat to these hopes. What could she do against the Roman empire? She hardly had any weapons other than those she used against Caesar, Antony and, in vain Octavius, the futur Augustus. To paraphrase a famous statement, "The heart has its reasons . . . of State."

A great excavation in the heart of the City of London unearths the temple of Mithra

5

n the cruel destruction of the present, wars sometimes lay bare the buried pages of history. Archaeologists get results in this way even if they wish for completely different methods of investigation. In Germany, the annihilation of the center of Cologne led to great discoveries. In France, the destruction of whole quarters and of houses in Marseille, Strasbourg and Amiens opened up an important field of research on the ancient past of these cities. In England, the bombing of London brought to light the remains of "Londinium", Roman London. Most of these were in the City and were buried under sizeable buildings, with no hope of their ever being found.

In 1954, a big company contracted to construct on a bomb site an office block of fourteen storeys. This site, known as Bucklersbury House, is in the heart of the City, between two well-known streets. One of these streets is Victoria Street which goes from Blackfriars Bridge to Mansion House—the Lord-Mayor's residence—and to the Royal Exchange. The other is Cannon Street which leads directly from St. Paul's Cathedral to London Bridge and to the Tower, the famous Tower of London.

These two streets are intersected by Walbrook, an artery named after a now extinct river, like the Bièvre or the stream of the Grange-Batelière in Paris. This stream, which of course flowed in Roman times, was known to have played an important role. During the last century, the remains of a large ancient building were found on its banks, but unfortunately the explorations were not continued because of roadworks and the construction of buildings. Nevertheless, when Queen Victoria Street was built across old London in 1869, a great Roman mosaic was among other things, discovered.

So the 14-storeyed block was to be built on a site laden with archaeological promise. They had to dig deep to lay the foundations. If remains lay hidden in the earth, they would inevitably be dug up by the bulldozers. The "Roman and Mediaeval London Excavation Council", always on the lookout for fragments of London's past, kept a vigilant eye on the site. It had assigned an excavation team to work there, led by W. F. Grimes, a great

specialist on antiquity, today a university professor of Archaeology, assisted by his wife, an
archaeologist too, and with the collaboration of
Norman Cook, the present custodian of the Guild
Museum.

The findings arouse great public interest

One can imagine that research carried out in
such conditions is very difficult. Even if the
contractors were respectful of the relics of the
past, they were obliged to work to a binding time-
limit, and there was the risk that the machines
used would irreparably damage what is of
archaeological interest.

W. F. Grimes' team were granted a time-limit
by the building contractors to carry out excavations. This limit was about to expire, when the
remains of a large building appeared. Were they to
abandon the digging, however difficult and un-
spectacular that would have seemed? On Sep-
tember 18, a very fine sculpture was unearthed:
a lifesize male head wearing a Phrygian cap.
That was a certain indication of the worship of
Mithra, this god who came from the mountains
of Phrygia and who was venerated throughout the
Roman Empire. Moreover, during the last century,
there came to light in those parts a Mithraic relief,
presented by a certain Ulpius Silvanius, a veteran
of the second legion Augusta which was garrisoned in England.

In fact the building, dug up by the Excavation Council, turned out to be a temple of Mithra. It was a fine stone building about 19 yards by 6½. It looked like the ground plan of a nave, flanked by two aisles, and ending in an apse to the west. Inside the apse was a raised platform to support an altar. One could have equally supposed it to be an early Christian building, when such an arrangement was common. Of course, this was not an imposing ruin to look at, nor did the walls still stand high. But how moving were these vestiges! They came out of the bottom of a giant excavation site, dominated by skyscrapers amongst bulldozers and cranes, and stood as battered but eloquent witnesses of a distant past and of a powerful and secret religion.

Immediately, the discovery provoked an immense reaction of curiosity. It was resoundingly echoed by the press, and Londoners, so closely attached to the history of their city, wanted to see the site. Such pressure was brought to bear by public opinion, that visits had to be organized which the contractors just as much as the archaeologists could have well done without. A touring-circuit was improvised, bounded by ropes. The thronging crowd made a strange spectacle forming interminable queues which spread into the neighboring streets. As a result, ten thousand visitors were recorded on the first day, fifteen thousand on the second. At first, the site was only open one hour, but during the last days, in order to meet the unceasing demand, visitors were admitted all the afternoon from 2.30 to 6.30.

The initiative taken by the Excavation Council deserves to be quoted as an exemple. The organization of these visits could only interfere with the research but, in its capacity as corporate body accountable for the city's past, it felt a duty to acquaint the public with these discoveries. One knows that the presence of crowds is not favorable to archaeological work but it also happens some-times that the latter is carried out with an exag-gerated secrecy, far from public view. Is there not a duty to make excavation sites as accessible as possible to the public? By this research, great pages of national history are revealed. The interest of the greatest possible number of people should be aroused.

Before this important discovery, the contrac-tors made a commendable decision, which was hardly compatible with their interests: they agreed to suspend work for a fortnight, so as to enable the excavating to continue. For a while, it was hoped to protect these remains and to keep them under the big building which was to be constructed. Unfortunately, this solution was not possible, for it would have been very costly and would have led to great technical problems.

The archaeologists still had a few surprises ahead of them. In front of the nave, sculptures were unearthed, arranged as if to be stored, in particular two magnificent heads. One, believed to be Minerva, is in grey marble. The top of the head is mutilated, but there are two holes, apparently to attach a diadem or a helmet, perhaps in bronze. The other is of Serapis. The noble face of this god, forcefully executed, though with a thoughtful use of relief, is framed by luxurious hair and a thick beard. The head bears a kind of cylindrical flowerpot, decorated with olive branches, which is none other than a "modius", that is, a measure of volume, which was used especially for wheat. This is by no means all that was discovered in this temple to Mithra. In addition, there was a small statue, no doubt of Mercury; a group in marble representing Dionysus-Bacchus, surrounded by a satyr, a maenad, a panther and the classic Silene sitting on an ass; a marble hand which must have belong to a very big statue, for it is twice as large as life; a fragment of a sculpture in relief of the lower part of a male body, holding an inverted torch. This is one of the two followers of the god Mithra, Cautopates, whose lowered torch symbolized night and death, while the other one, representing day and life, held his torch upright.

This is not the place to compile a catalogue of objects that were found. Excepting Cautopates, which is a provincial work carried out in England, all the sculptures are in Italian marble, and there is no doubt that they come from workshops in the Peninsula. At least two of them may be called masterpieces: the one supposed to represent Minerva and the Serapis. The latter strongly resembles a sculpture which is at the Museum of the Vatican and is considered to be the copy of the work of the famous Greek sculptor, Bryaxis.

A curious gathering of gods

This curious gathering of divinities greatly intrigued the archaeologists in London, who had really not been able to provide a satisfactory answer to the problem raised. Serapis originated from an Egyptian god, who was later confused with Jupiter and Pluto. The London bust shows him in the latter form, the symbol of fertility of the earth. Mercury was the protector of merchants and travelers, and this earned him his well-known attributes: the caduceus, the winged sandals, as well as the purse, symbolizing the gains of commerce. Dionysus-Bacchus was the god of wine, of inspiration and of mystical frenzy—hence the usual train of satyrs, drunkenly perched on donkeys, maenads and divine Bacchants. Minerva, on the other end, was of a purely intellectual nature that is, if it is truly herself who is portrayed.

It was customary for Roman gods to live next to one another and to get on well together. But in London, they were crowded together, an improbable thing to find in a temple to Mithra, when one remembers that the worship of the Phrygian god was very exclusive, and in any case, far removed from the Graeco-Roman pantheon.

Why is it then that these sculptures, which seem on the whole to date from the 2nd century

A.D., should be found gathered together in this place? A first hypothesis is that, in the later period of Roman rule, the temple of Mithra became a kind of "All Saints'" chapel, in which the most diverse of gods were gathered together pell-mell and worshipped. The cult of Mithra mainly involved rich merchants and officers of the Roman army, that is to say, men who held real power. Pagan gods were better sheltered in this sanctuary in the face of growing Christianity.

This hypothesis is certainly attractive but untenable. Indeed it is a striking thing that the sculptures should be found piled together in a very small space and that, on the other hand, they should be on the whole in excellent condition. An obvious explanation is that, when most of the country had been converted to Christianity, these images of god were hidden, so as not to be destroyed, in the temple of Mithra. There they were safer, because those who protected them held high positions. This is perhaps how these sacred objects were laid up, either by Romans or by Romanized natives, whether they remained faithful to their old gods, or whether, even though converted to Christianity, they reserved them secret favors.

The kouros, of the archaic period, discovered at Piraeus.
Photograph by Boudot-Lemotte

The temple of Zeus at Olympia. Broken columns and remains of fallen buil
give evidence of the past splendor of the monument. *Photograph Seymour-Ma*

A religion founded in Iran invades the Roman empire

The discovery of a temple of Mithra in the heart of London added an element of capital importance to the history of the propagation of the Mithraic faith in the Roman empire. This is not the first sanctuary to be uncovered in ancient Britain. There have been three others—at Borcovicium (Housesteads), Brocolita (Carrawburgh) and Vindobala—but they were in a military zone on the northern borders. This can be explained by the propagation of Mithraism among the legionaries. The London temple is the first to be discovered.

It is not intented here to draw up a treatise on this cult which played such an important part in the development of religious ideas in Roman times. But a few words are necessary here. The Mithraic faith originated in the vicinity of Iran and is closely related to Zoroastrianism. The Roman legions became acquainted with it when they set foot in Asia Minor and ardently spread it, probably because there was a true affinity between the military spirit and that of this religion, which preached exertion and demanded great courage and real physical trials for initiation, which was reserved solely for men. It also advocated an organized hierarchy and strict discipline.

A salutary and perfectly moral religion, Mithraism spread with extraordinary vigor throughout the Roman empire and Renan's famous phrase has often been quoted, "If Christianity had been checked in its growth by a fatal disease, the world would have become Mithraic." The initiates were grouped into fraternities, with initiation rites which have been compared with those of the Freemasons. They met usually in small chapels, for they were few in number.

The temple of Carrawburgh by Hadrian's Wall, excavated in 1950, was, therefore, only a little more than 12 yards long. That of London was bigger, 21 yards long, as we have already noted. The dates of this monument have been determined. It was built in the middle of the 2nd century, as is shown by a coin of the emperor Hadrian, which was discovered in the foundations. It underwent various modifications and was still in existence at the beginning of the 4th century. We know this from a coin of Constantine the Great, who was emperor from 306 to 337.

An object of particular interest, and of great artistic value as well, was found during the digging. It had been placed in the north wall of the temple, probably hidden there at the same time as the group of divine images. It is a silver box of a late period which, in all likelihood, was used in Mithraic rites. This receptacle is decorated entirely with reliefs forming an admirable frieze, mainly of fighting scenes, between men, men and animals, and animals against animals. It is worthy of notice that the fauna is, on the whole, African: elephants, lions, hippopotami, a crocodile and snakes. But there are also fabulous animals:

griffins with an eagle's head and wings, and a lion's body. Two of them hold—and are apparently trying to open—kinds of cages. Other scenes show a man emerging from such a cage.

The last depiction is perplexing. Some have imagined it to be the symbolization of a Christian being tormented. Perhaps it is more likely to be the representation of a rite peculiar to the cult of Mithra: the simulacrum of death and resurrection, which played an important part in the Mithraic initiation. But it is striking that, in the mosaic of the Great Chase, at Piazza Armerina, Sicily, there is a similar scene: a griffin resting its paw on a barred cage, in which a man is enclosed. These two scenes are strangely similar, but this comparison does not, for all that, provide the key to this enigmatic and curious representation.

An outraged queen's revolt

The discovery of the temple of Mithra would have been quite enough for the London archaeologists. From the gaping pits in the heart of the City, however, they were to lift other veils of the history of ancient London. Remains of Roman structures and roads enabled them to map more perfectly the way things must have stood in the first few centuries A.D. What is more, they were able to identify the "Cripplegate Fort" which occupied the north-west quarter of the City. This turned out to be a great edifice covering at least

10 acres. It would seem to have been built at the end of the 1st century or the beginning of the 2nd. Later, it was incorporated into the vast system of fortifications which encircled the town.

Events of British history come alive through these military vestiges, and are surrounded by an aura of legendary national heroism, even if they are clouded by acts of cruelty and by a certain melancholy. When the "Cripplegate Fort" was built, London was rising up from its ruins—a mere heap of rubble, thick with corpses. Boadicea's revolt had passed through there. Boadicea is inscribed as a great heroine in the pages of history, and her role deserves to be mentioned.

It is known that Britain—the name "England" cannot yet be used—was conquered by the Romans as late as 43, that is after the conquest of Mauritania. This was a great adventure for Rome, for the island was, in Tacitus' startling words, "the remotest land and the last outpost of freedom."

The Icenic people inhabited the south-east part of the island. Their king, Prositagus, had accepted the suzerainty of Rome. He died during the winter of 60-61, leaving no male heirs. Nero, then emperor, did not trouble himself with legal or sentimental contingencies. The death of this king was a good opportunity to eliminate his family, to transform his territories into a single Roman province and to confiscate his goods. Boadicea, Prositagus' widow, was whipped, and outrages were carried on her two daughters. At the same time, the local aristocracy was dispossessed of the loans the emperor Claudius had granted.

The revolt broke out in a blaze of fury. Boadicea headed it, and not only the Iceni but the neighboring people, the Trinobantes, followed her without hesitation for, according to Tacitus, among the Britons "no distinction of sex is made in leadership." Boadicea was queen, military leader and also a priestess, and it is perhaps to this very religious prestige that she owed most of her power. The Latin historian Dion Cassius relates that, before heading an expedition, she mounted a tribune, seized a spear and stirred up her troops at length, then unleashed a hare whose running was a good omen. She finished by an invocation to Victory, the goddess of the nation, and, of course, by a violent diatribe against Nero and the Romans.

This is surely a splendid subject for imagery of the type used by Epinal. Boadicea is said to have commanded as many as 120,000 warriors. First she descended on Camulodunum, near the east coast, north of the Thames, today Colchester. The Romans had made it their first provincial capital and established there a nucleus of veteran soldiers. The town fell after barely two days and the prisoners were massacred without quarter. The legate, Suetonius Paulinus, who had nevertheless proved himself in the African campaign defeating the tribes of the Atlas mountains, found himself confronted with an almost desperate situation. He considered London indefensible and evacuated it.

The future mercantile and financial vocation of London

The town fell in massacre and fire, and the amount of ashes found in the layers under the ground enables us to measure the scale of the disaster. Paulinus chose his battle ground. Not only were there available but 10,000 men but also they were very poorly organized: just one legion, to which were joined auxiliary foot-soldiers and horsemen. On the other side, the Britons lined up in contingents eight times superior in number. Boadicea exhorted her soldiers, inspected their ranks in a chariot, her two daughters on either side of her. But the Iceni, poorly armed, lacked both training and discipline and, hampered by "impedimenta", were soon routed. So sure had they been of victory that their families followed in carts. The battle was hideous and confirmed and hesitant rebels alike perished by sword and fire. Boadicea is said to have poisoned herself. Another version has it that she died of illness soon after the battle.

When peace had returned, London recovered from its ruins and the building of Cripplegate Fort, which was mentioned earlier, dates from this period of restoration. Actually, this town was so well placed that it could never fall. Ships arrived in its river port, and a vast network of roads spread out from Londinium. It has been found that the system of railroads, of which London is the center, follows roughly that traced out by Roman road builders. If the conquerors had originally intended to govern the province from Camulodunum (Colchester), the seat of financial administration was rapidly moved to London. At the dawn of our era, London had already established its mercantile and financial vocation, in which it has never ceased to surpass itself throughout the centuries. Towards the fall of the empire, it was to be not only the provincial treasury but also the residence of the civil governor, who presided over the destinies of the whole country.

It was said earlier that Cripplegate Fort was part of the vast wall which surrounded the town and which assured it an area as great as its importance. It was spread over 320 acres, a considerable area.

A mine of treasure in a little stream

Just as the Phoenix, that fabulous bird, was burnt at the stake and was reborn out of his ashes, so London has always proudly risen up from its ruins. Under Hadrian's rule, the town was completely burned down, as it was to be 15 centuries later in 1666. The site of an agglomeration so often destroyed and rebuilt poses serious problems for archaeologists. So do cities teeming with life, where the distant past has been literally effaced by acts of destruction.

A river bed has yielded many important findings, that of the little Walbrook, which flowed through the Roman town and which no longer exists. This stream served as a garbage dump where endless objects were lost or thrown away. Archaeologists have reaped there a rich and important harvest. The material collected can be seen in the London Museum and, especially, in the Guildhall Museum which, since the Second World War, has been moved to the Royal Exchange, in the very heart of the City.

These objects stand as moving witnesses to the daily life of Londoners of antiquity, and particularly to their activities and trades. In this way, a lot of writing-material was found in the Walbrook, and this is worth delving into in detail. For it involves a most complete range of means used in antiquity: from the styli, in bronze and iron, often remarkably worked, and the wooden tablets on which they engraved, to the inkwell and the quill-pen with pointed tip, of modern design, which was used to write on parchment and papyrus. There is evidence that considerable quantities of papyrus were imported from Egypt.

Among these last objects were discovered some very curious documents. A tablet bears a circular imprint, which is an administrative stamp: PROC AVG DEDERVNT BRIT PROV translatable by, "Issued by the imperial procurators of the Province of Briton."

A brief greeting to friends

But another tablet, dating probably from the 1st century, bears a most informal message. On the outside, it reads: LONDINIO—London. The text is written in cursive handwriting on the inside surface. Perhaps the reader will be entertained by this transcription: *Rufus Callisuni salutem Epillico et omnibus contubernalibus certiores vos esse credo me recte valere si vos indicem fecistis rogo mittite omnia diligenter cura agas ut illam puellam ad nummum redigas....* It says roughly this, "Rufus, son of Callisunus, sends his greetings to Epillicus and all the comrades. I think you know that I am very well. If you have made the inventory, please take care to send all of it. See to the receipt of the money that this girl is worth." In a few lines, he greets his friends, gives news of his health and issues business instructions, to the end of collecting money from the sale of a young slave girl.

Among the objects found, there is an astonishing range of tools, which bring alive the many trades busy in the Roman city: carpenters, masons, locksmiths, furriers and many others. Looking at the glass-cases, one may reflect on the permanence of tools or, even more on the fact that, as far back as those ancient days, their forms had already been definitely established, and would hardly change during the centuries that followed.

Consider an oak ladder, found in a well, dating from the 1st century A.D. 15 feet long, it is intact and all the rungs are in place. Were it not for the fine patina of its wood, it would look like one from any cheap store in the present City. Consider also a wicker basket, such as peasant women today carry, some sandals and leather panties—a "bikini"—which were tied in two knots around the hips.

Whether one ponders on a temple evocative of strange rites and containing magnificent sculptures, or on small objects of trade, dress and everyday life, all these things constitute the patrimony of a city and of a civilization. It is the task—and the pride—of archaeology to discover and interpret it and, in so doing, to reconstitute history.

A fabulous treasure of silver in the ancient city of Augst, near Basel

bout 6 miles to the west of Basel, in Augst, there lies one of the most imposing collections that antiquity has ever left us. Swiss archaeologists excavated and restored it extremely methodically. One after the other, splendid monuments came to light, in the serene setting of undulating countryside, with mountains as a background.

"Augusta Raurica" was the name of this town, at the same time recalling the emperor and the Rauric people on whose territory it was built.

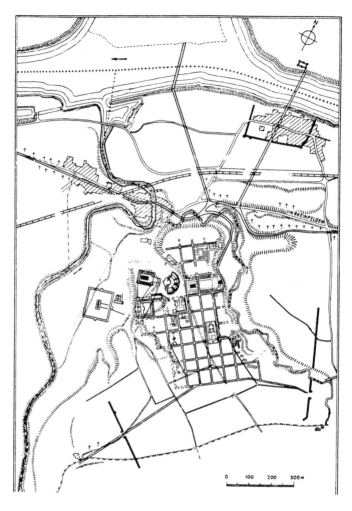

Map of Augusta Raurica. Above right, on the banks of the Rhine, the Roman *castrum* of Kaiseraugst, today almost entirely covered over by a village. In 1961, the treasure of silver was found in the south-west corner of the surrounding wall. Map drawn by A. Wildberger for the Pro Augusta Raurica *Foundation*.

A sister town of Lyon

It had been founded as a colony, in 44 B.C., by Munatius Plancus, a lieutenant of Caesar, at the same time as Lyon. Gaul had just been conquered, but Barbarians still constituted a threat on the Rhine frontier. "Raurica" was an outpost, a place of observation and a citadel, near the great bend of the river. Yet Rome's power made itself felt there through its imposing architecture, a most effective psychological tactic for still restive populations. In fact, the town was built out of nothing on a grandiose scale, and is a perfect example of Roman town planning, with its wide intersecting streets, marking out spacious residential areas, its enormous forum with the basilica and curia, its temples, theater, amphitheater and baths.

During the 1st and 2nd centuries, when Roman peace was at its height, Augusta Raurica prospered, even though it was not very populated, in great luxury, as the excavations attest. But it was doomed by its very position, a key point on the Rhine. At the beginning of the 3rd century, it suffered the first attack of the Alamans. In an attempt to defend itself, ramparts were begun but were never completed, probably because they had to surround too vast an area. The town was to suffer ruin upon ruin by a renewed Alaman wave in 260. This was the town's death-knell.

But the Roman power could not afford to abandon such a key position. The stones of the half-dead city, ofits tottering monuments, were then used to build, on the banks of the Rhine itself and at the northern extremity of Augst, a fortified camp commanding a bridge, which was protected by an advanced post on the north bank. This is the "Castrum Rauricense".

The date of this "castrum" is questionable. History and archaeology suggest that it was built at the end of the 3rd century under Diocletian. He energetically reorganized the Roman army and reinforced the Rhine frontier, bordering it with forts and supporting positions, which ensured him advanced posts—such as existed at Mayence-Kastell and Cologne-Deutz. In any case, the fortress built at Augst was strong and fearful. It had the shape of a trapezium, 300 yards on its longer side and 155 yards wide. The surrounding wall was over 4 yards thick—major portions are still in evidence—and it was flanked by more than 30 massive projecting towers, square in shape. A legion—the "Legio 1 Martia"—came to be garrisoned there.

An enormous mass of stone was used to build this stronghold. Since needs had to be met as quickly as possible, materials from the buildings of Raurica were mainly used. There have been found debris of buildings, sculptures and inscriptions, all buried in this mass. These were dark days of the Empire, when the necessities of defense brought about the sacrifice of the monuments which had at its weight stood as proud symbols of the might of Rome.

On a winter's day in 1961

Excavating at Augst dates back to the 16th century when a humanist and a scholar of that period began research there. Their names deserve a place of honor, among ancestors, in the golden book of archaeology. Methodical exploration of the site was taken up again at the end of the last century. Today it has gained fresh and crucial momentum under the leadership of an eminent Swiss specialist, Rudolf Laur-Belart, a professor at the University of Basel and the director of the "Pro Augusta Raurica" foundation.

The "Castrum", built at a late date, its purpose as well as its style being completely military, had to be relegated to a secondary importance in the program of research Moreover, it is difficult to explore. Its site is almost entirely covered by a village, Kaiseraugst, and this name reminds us that until 1803 it was imperial territory. Besides, the Swiss archaeologists felt a duty to expend effort and money especially on this Roman town, the soil of which was certain to yield monuments and living-quarters, together with a whole retinue of art objects made when the Empire was at its height. Kaiseraugst was above all important for the study and knowledge of a Roman stronghold at the decline of the Empire. Apart from that, great revelations were not to be expected.

And yet at the end of 1961, just after Christmas, an extraordinary discovery was to take place inside Kaiseraugst at the foot of the ramparts,

whose rugged construction had partially with-
stood the ravages of time and of men. Thus the
somewhat gloomy faces lit up with surprise at
the unexpected finding. Once again chance,
the providence of archaeologists, had truly intervened.

At the end of this year 1961, the building of a
school gymnasium had been begun on the south-
west corner of the former fortress, where a farm-
house had been. On December 27, a bulldozer
began churning up the earth, mainly in a area
formerly crossed by the Roman path which followed the inside wall. Much earth had been dug up
when it broke down. How fortunate it is—as will
be seen—that mechanical failures sometimes
happen! Meanwhile snow fell continuously for
several hours, and was 16 inches deep on the site.

In mid-January, the weather became milder
and a thaw set in. This was a godsend for the
children. The heaps of earth and the snow pits
made a good place to play in. One Sunday, a man
from Basel strolled by. He perceived a metal object
protruding from a heap of rubble and, intrigued,
he strove to pull it out, but it was stuck in the frozen
earth. The following day, he went to find Professor
Belart and told him what he had seen. He thought
it was a great silver plate. It was indeed lucky
that the bulldozer had broken down. The object
was still there. There was no doubt about it. It was
silver and of Roman origin.

Immediately, Rudolf Laur-Belart and his colla-
borators began work. They unearthed other

objects, brought specialists of the Swiss army with mine detectors and, at the same time, made enquiries in the village as to whether metal objects had been found on the site. Prudently, of course, silver was not mentioned.

Then it was learned that a nine year old boy had been collecting plates and had been piling them up. He had taken some to his teacher who, in a bad mood that day, had told him to go and take this scrap iron to the nearest garbage dump. One woman said that she had retrieved five plates and put them away in a barn, but she hastened to give them to the Museum of Augst. A rare object had been thrown into a heap of manure.

Professor Laur-Belart carried out his research in the worst conditions and with patient perseverance, stopping work on March 8, 1962, certain that the earth had nothing more to yield. The research had been very fruitful. The treasure totalled 255 objects, including the medals and coins.

The catalog of treasures

The treasure consists solely of objects in pure silver, often touched up in gold, some chiselled with fine decorations. This is not the place to describe them in detail, but at least a list can be made: 6 large plates—one of them is no less than 24$\frac{1}{2}$ inches in diameter; one rectangular plate, copiously ornamented; 3 bowls, 2 fish platters, 4 cups, 4 goblets, spoons and other eating-utensils, a splendid candelabra—4 feet high, a little statuette of Venus, seventeen large medals, one hundred and sixty coins and three ingots.

As can be seen, the collection is quite varied. It is no extraordinary thing that it should consist mainly of eating-utensils. On the contrary, most Roman discoveries in various countries consist of these. The most important objects, and the finest too, are of Eastern origin, as will be seen later on. In this the treasure of Kaiseraugst is no exception. And in any case, if only for the weight in silver, this treasure must have belonged to a very important personage. The first thing that comes to mind is an emperor. Different hypotheses can be advanced on this subject, and here they are.

The finest object of the treasure is an octagonal plate, 21 inches wide, and weighing 12 lb. 8 oz. The artist's signature is on the base in Greek: Pausylypos Thessalonika. The central medallion and the edges are decorated with finely chiselled scenes in relief. One does not have to be a great scolar in mythology to identify the subject. It consists of the main scenes of the childhood and youth of Achilles.

The brave Achilles had many adventures. Homer made him popular in his "Iliad" and, later, poets did not want to be left out of things. In the center of the plate found at Kaiseraugst is a well-known scene: the ruse Ulysses used to lure

Achilles from his hiding-place. This spicey story is well-known. The young and handsome Achilles is peacefully hidden in the court of the king Lycomedes; he is dressed in women's clothes and is called Pyrrha (Achilles the Redhead). Not a bit bothered by his disguise, he becomes involved with one of the king's daughters and lives with her. Unfortunately, this was not to last. Ulysses had learned that Troy could not be taken without Achilles' help. He succeeded in finding his hiding-place and entered the women's quarters. There, he started sounding a trumpet. This was enough to arouse Achilles' fighting instincts. The latter demanded weapons and, Ulysses having taken care to bring some, heeding only his courage, he went off to carry out his duty.

The artist Pausylypos has treated this famous scene well. Achilles can be seen brandishing a shield and a spear. One of the king's daughters— probably the beautiful Deidamia, who bore him a child—tries in vain to hold him back. This time his mind is made up: he is going off to war. His male instincts have returned to him, but he is still dressed in light and flowing women's clothes which, worse, expose a generous breast. He has gone too far in the transvestite role. One can see, by this, that mythology has some very compromising situations.

On the circumference of the plate, other scenes of the hero's youth are portrayed, although a few liberties have been taken. There is another famous episode. So as to make him invulnerable, the hero's mother plunges the little Achilles in the waters of the Styx, the infernal river; to do this, she immerses him headfirst, holding him by one heel which, untouched by the magic water, remains vulnerable. This is to bring about the death of the hero who is struck down in that part by the fatal arrow. On the Kaiseraugst plate, this scene is portrayed with a curious detail: Achilles' mother holds him by two legs, in order to plunge him in the Styx. According to this, the hero would be vulnerable in both heels, which does not conform to the tradition. Fewer things are better chiselled or more interesting to study than this legend of Achilles, interpreted by Pausylypos of Thessalonika, whose name and talent become known to us in this discovery at Kaiseraugst.

Professor Laur-Belart made a very interesting comparison, conducive to our knowing the owner of the plate. He recalled that Basilina, the mother of Julian the Apostate, who was to wear the imperial purple in 361, had a strange dream before the birth of the future emperor: she dreamed that she was going to give birth to Achilles. Perhaps the artist was trying to recall Julian the Apostate through the legend of the hero. This is an hypothesis to be dealt with later on.

Another big plate, 17 inches in diameter, is also signed, this time in Latin: EVTICIUS NAISI. This artist was a native of the ancient city—today Nish in south-east Jugoslavia—where the emperor Constantine was born. Another plate, gilded and inlaid with niello, 23 inches in diameter, displays a central medallion, and this etching is exceedingly clever, though overcrowded. The subject remains a mystery to this day. There is portrayed a fortified town, where opulent buildings rise, with Corinthian columns, pediments and cupolas. The sea is all around, and lovers are fishing in boats, and the water is so teeming with fish and octopuses that the catch must have been plentiful.

But the whole treasure cannot be described here in detail. Worthy of note, however, is some curious cutlery, of a shape that was until now unknown. It must have been used for delicacies and especially for shell-fish and snails. It is strange that one of them bears the monogram: X P. This is the only evidence of Christianity in the whole treasure. But it remains a mystery as to why it should be found on these bizarre and luxurious instruments.

The imperial genealogy at the Empire's decline

All this silver bears the mark of the 4th century A.D. But the date of the treasure is made more precise by the medallions and coins which are included in it. These are so well preserved that they appear fresh from the mint, and bear the effigies of Constantine I—sometimes known as Constantine the Great—, of his sons, Constant I and Constance II. The three heavy ingots contained in the treasure have the effigy of the usurper Magnence.

The synoptic table which follows should be referred to. It summarizes the imperial family tree in the middle of the 4th century and, admittedly, it is somewhat complicated. Constantine, Constant, Constance—this is enough to discourage those not familiar with Roman history. This was a dark period, if ever there was one, when brother killed brother for the possession of the Empire. There was an usurper too. Crimes, suicides, murderous fights between brothers, "pronunciamentos" and violent acts were to the fore, whilst the barbaric hordes were in the background.

Constantine—the same who granted Christianity a free rein—died in 337, after moving the imperial capital to Byzance, which he named after himself. He ruled for nearly 30 years. The historian and archaeologist Jean-Jacques Hatt wrote, "His actions were as excellent and spectacular in their primary results as they were disastrous in their more far-reaching consequences. He was one of those monarchs, like Louis XIV, who burned and withered by their setting rays more intensely than they warmed at their apoges."

Before his death, Constantine divided the Empire among his 3 sons. One of them, Constant, is entrusted with the eastern empire, and proved himself to be a good enough monarch. But in 350, when he was out hunting one day, a military putsch broke out, and the Imperial purple was usurped by a senior officer, Magnence, who was born at Amiens of a Briton father and a Frankish mother. He was one of those "barbarians", to whom the Empire unwisely entrusted senior military positions. He commanded 2 choice legions. The emperor Julian—the Apostate—, who was to reign ten years later, wrote of him, "He despised the Empire to the point of usurping it in the reek of drunkenness and wine . . . He was the murderer of his own master (Constant I was killed at Elne near the Pyrenees by an emissary of Magnence), and he wants to command us, he who could not even have considered himself a free man, if he had not obtained from us this right!" These are revengeful words of a Roman against an impudent soldier of fortune. Today, some historians paint a less sinister picture of him. However that may be, he was soon recognized by a part of the Empire—Gaul, Spain and Africa—, and he gained mastery of Rome. After three and a half years of rule, he was routed by Constance, Constantine the Great's other son to whom the eastern empire had fallen, and he committed suicide at Lyon.

This usurper's reign, although short-lived, was marked by an abundant coinage of high quality, on which it pleased Magnence to display all the titles he had arrogated to himself. Now, he was plagued with financial difficulties and precious metal were becoming rare. The great numismatist, Jean Babelon, to whom we owe an excellent study of Magnence, as seen through his issued coins, asserts, "For the usurper, more than anyone else, coinage was the symbol of sovereign power, the confirmation of his authority and the best instrument of propaganda.''

Whoever has the good fortune to hold in his hand the heavy ingots—which each weigh 3 Roman pounds or about 2 lb.—cannot but vividly imagine this reign of Magnence, characterized by a borrowed and, what is more, bloodstained purple, as if it were a discarded garment of the theater.

Who owned the treasure?

We must now attempt to answer the questions which first come to mind. To whom did the treasure belong? How and when was it hidden?

The circumstances of the discovery did not help to determine this. The bulldozer which ploughed up the site did not facilitate the drawing of useful conclusions which, besides, could hardly have thrown light on anything but the hiding-place itself. And in any case, this had not been built in strong materials. At best, the treasure had been buried in a wooden box. It has been proven that the hiding of such objects was done carelessly, either because serious and pressing events required this, or because the holder did not wish to draw attention.

One may easily imagine some sinister drama. The treasure could only have belonged to an important personage who gathered wealth during the height of his power. One day, he and his

EMPERORS AND USURPERS
IN THE MIDDLE OF THE 4th CENTURY

•

CONSTANTIN I, called THE GREAT
emperor from 306 to 337; divides the Empire between
his three children:

1 — CONSTANTIN II, called THE YOUNG
born at Arles, emperor from 337 to 350. Defeated and
killed near Aquileia when trying to seize the states of
his brother, Constant I.

2 — CONSTANT I
emperor from 337 to 350. Ruled the western empire.
Killed at Elne by an emissary of the usurper, Magnence
(see below)

3 — CONSTANCE II
emperor from 337 to 361. Ruled the eastern empire.
Sole emperor after 351. On his accession he had
massacred the two brothers of his father and their
descendants, with the exception of Julian, who was
later to be proclaimed emperor (see below).

•

MAGNENCE
usurping emperor, proclaimed at Autun in 350. He tried
to be on friendly terms with Constance II and to share
the Empire with him; he is finally defeated near Gap
and commits suicide in 353 at Lyon. Conferred to his
brother Decence the title of Caesar and entrusted him
with the defence of the borders of Gaul. But Decence
was beaten by the allied Franks and Alamans, and
committed suicide in 353 at Sens.

•

JULIAN, called THE APOSTATE
was summoned by his cousin, Constance II to save Gaul
from its Germanic invaders. He defeated them in the
region of Strasbourg. Proclaimed emperor by the
troop in Paris, in 361, he reigned till 363, at which date
he was killed during a campaign in Persia.

retinue were seized by a great panic. This treasure of Kaiseraugst weighs a great deal, yet it could have been contained in a bag and loaded on to a cart or even a good horse. For it to have been thus hidden in haste, the situation must have been particularly dangerous, with a terrifying enemy beating at the doors. In history, there are many examples of fleeing troops leaving behind their weapons rather than their goods, especially when the latter were valuable. The dramatic flavor is heightened by the fact that neither the owner of all this wealth nor a right-hand man was ever able to return to the hiding-place. He must have died thinking of the riches that had been a mark of his power.

The misfortune which led to the concealment of the treasure at Kaiseraugst could not, of course, have occurred before 350, the date at which Magnence, whose effigy the ingots bear, seized power. It must have taken place a few years later, for the treasure contains no coins of emperors later than the usurper. This calls to mind the great invasion of 352, and recent archaeological discoveries, notably in Alsace, have confirmed its importance. Magnence, who began by trying to establish friendly terms with Constant, left for Italy to make war against him. He entrusted the defense of the Rhine frontier to his brother Decence, an adventurer on whom he had conferred the title of Caesar, under these circumstances. This was a good opportunity for barbarians to strike. Constant, the legitimate emperor, and Magnence, the usurper, devastated one another, bringing with them troops which would have done better to stay in the region of the Rhine. The Franks and the Alamans formed a coalition and gained a decisive victory over Decence. This is believed to have taken place between Bingen and Mainz. They destroyed about 40 towns and captured the northeast of Gaul, including Alsace. It was probably then that the barbarians crossed the Rhine, and, it is thought, destroyed the major role of Kaiseraugst as a key stronghold. Decence could well have stowed away his treasure there, considering it to be safer there than in a fortress on the lower Rhine.

The treachery of General Barbation

Another hypothesis may be based on events which occurred five years later. Constance II summoned his cousin Julian, who was later proclaimed emperor and set down in history as Julian—the Apostate—in an attempt to save the situation on the Rhine. In 357, Julian began a vigorous campaign. Starting at Saverne, he attacked the barbarians, while the leader of the cavalry, Barbation, at the head of 25,000 men, had the mission of closing in on the region of Basel. Unfortunately, Barbation felt a real hatred towards Julian and disobeyed his orders. Under a surprise attack from the Alamans, he was pushed back in great confusion as far as Basel and it is

recorded that he lost a large part of his arms-
bearers and goods in the battle. It may therefore
be supposed that the precious deposit at Kaiseraugst is none other than the booty of war of the
fleeing general who, harassed by the enemy, was
seized with panic and hid it in haste.

The treason of Barbation was not, however, to
prevent Julian from gaining a decisive victory
over the Alamans near Strasbourg. The hypothesis of Professor Laur-Belart is worthy of
mention, at this point. He suggests that the
decoration on this magnificent plate could describe the youth of Julian the Apostate. If this is
so, it may be conjectured that it belonged to this
emperor and that he hid it at August, where he
stayed in 361, before leaving with his troops to
wage war against his cousin Constance. Julian
was never to return to Gaul, which had adopted
him and proclaimed him emperor. This would
explain why the treasure was never recovered.

These events of history are matter for reflec-
tion when one considers the treasure of Kaiseraugst. These lavish vessels are mute relics, which
it would be vain to interrogate. An attempt to
disperse their mystery necessarily evokes a whole
succession of historical figures, mainly conspir-
ators and brutal soldiers. There is a strange
contrast between the purity of the silver and the
vile deeds of those who may have owned it.

The mysterious treasure of the bronzes of Neuvy–en–Sullias

7

he little village of Neuvy-en-Sullias in the department of the Loiret seemed hardly destined for fame. Like thousands of other French villages, it led a peaceful and uneventful existence. However, it did have the privilege of being situated in the Loire valley which has an abundance of pleasant and gently undulating countryside.

One day, its name appeared in the headlines, not just as a record of fleeting sensationalism, but in longstanding and reputable journals which may be relied on for quality. In that district, an extraordinary treasure had just been found—the very mention of this word causes ecstasy among serious archaeologists and lovers of the fantastic alike.

Many sites of little interest have taken on an aura of fame after an archaeological discovery.

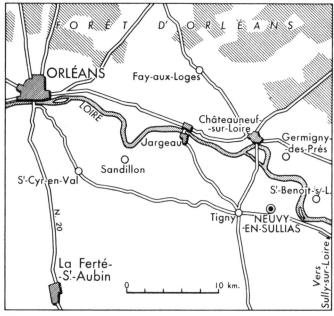

Map of the area surrounding Neuvy-en-Sullias. (To be translated in map): above, Forest of Orléans; *bottom right,* towards Sully-sur-Loire.

One of the most typical examples of this is the humble village of Vix near Châtillon-sur-Seine. It soon became immensely celebrated, when the famous "prince's" tomb was discovered. Many other cases exist. Just as humble families sometimes discover old documents in archives, conferring on them titles of nobility, so obscure villages have their prestige enhanced, when ancient objects are unearthed. There is thus an archaeological "lineage" which is being constantly added to. There has been a profusion of such chance discoveries, in places where the soil has remained undisturbed and has faithfully preserved the vestiges of the past.

The discovery at Neuvy-en-Sullias, about to be described, is not recent. It occurred a little over a hundred years ago, but surely, in dealing with archaeology, one may go back into the past; for a century is a small span when compared with millennia. Also the treasure, discovered in 1861, remained comparatively obscure for a long time, and was the concern of hardly anyone but specialists. It is only in recent years, that its artistic value has been recognized and praised. Treasures in gold and silver have an immutable prestige. That of Neuvy-en-Sullias is only in bronze, but the works of art which it contains must be evaluated from a purely aesthetic point of view. For a few decades, they were not only neglected, but also poorly judged. They do not, of course, conform to classical criteria, but today they are given an important place in the history of national art.

It happened in a sand quarry on May 27, 1861

Neuvy-en-Sullias can be found only on a detailed map. This village is situated on the south bank of the Loire, just under 2 miles, as the crow flies, upstream from Orléans. It is roughly opposite the two famous monuments, situated on the other bank: the church of Germigny-des-Prés, built under Charlemagne, and the abbot's house of Saint-Benoît-sur-Loire, one of the most remarkable existing Romanesque buildings. On the edge of Neuvy-en-Sullias, on the road—called the "nationale 751"—leading to the nearby village, Tigny, there was, on the lowlands where rye is grown, a field resembling a moor, evidence of the sandy alluvium in the Loire valley. It was completely barren land, though it was exploited as a sand quarry, which was an inward sloping semi-circle about 50 yards across and 2 or 3 deep. The workers progressed by pushing in the sides of the slope.

On May 27, 1861, seven workers were extracting sand. One of them felt something resist his pickaxe, while tackling the slope. Shortly, he worked loose a small wall made of uncemented bricks, which collapsed. A gaping hole then appeared. The seven workers gathered together and discussed this curious discovery. At first, they thought they had fallen on an old oven, and began trying to clear it.

All of a sudden, there was a strange apparition. An animal with a horse's head stood facing them.

Bust found at Cherchell, supposed to represent Cleopatra the Great. *Management of Algerian antiquities*

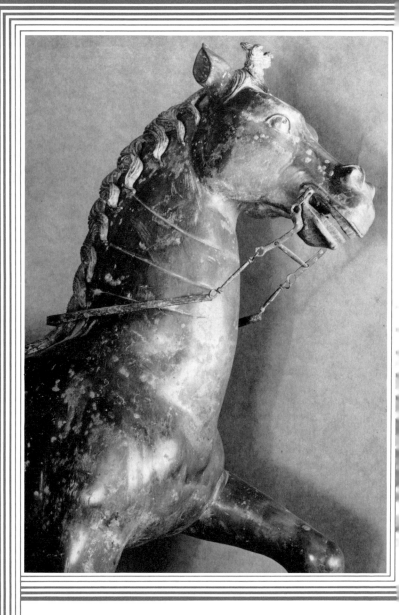

The horse bearing the inscription to Rudiobus. Height 3 ft. 6 ins.
Photograph by J. Boulas

It occurred to them that they had come upon a deposit of ancient objects, so they abandoned their picks and shovels and worked loose, with their hands, the magnificent bronze horse, which saw daylight at last after so many centuries. At the same time, a heap of objects appeared in the hiding-place: animals and human beings, varying in size, and on the whole in good condition.

At this point, it would be best to quote one of the first witnesses to the memorable discovery, P. Mantellier, the director of the Historical Museum of the district of Orléans.

"When all had been cleared, there was seen to be a pit 4 feet 6 inches square. In order to retain the sand, a wall of tile fragments had been built, with overlapping edges, held together neither by cement nor mortar. At the bottom, more tiles and some bricks had been laid to form the area on which stood the horse and the objects that were found next to it. A roof of boards had probably been placed on top, covered with a layer of earth. Little by little, the boards rotted and the layer of earth that they supported must have collapsed and become mixed up with the objects underneath. This happened haphazardly, without the whole forming a solid mass. This explains why the workers, who had begun by tackling one of the walls, had noticed that there were objects in the empty spaces not completely filled in by the earth and sand falling from above."

There was no doubt that this was a hiding place hurriedly built on this sandy moor where it was easy to dig. There must have been great haste to escape the sinister and approaching menace. It is easy to imagine the Loire as a scene of seething hordes of barbarians. There was no time to lose, and flight was imperative. The roads were unsafe and it was out of the question to load the precious goods on to a cart. It was, therefore, decided to bury them and to recover them in better days. One may well wonder what happened to those who kept the secret. Were they killed, or did they go so far away that they could not return? In any case, the deposit was to remain buried in the earth.

"How unbelievably ugly!..."

This made a good break for the workers who were used to shovelling sand and, all of a sudden, had a treasure on their hands. One of them wanted to share it out between them, when it came to light. But there were seven of them, and it was impossible to keep the secret. Now, the prefect of police had issued an order that all mayors should inform him of any ancient discoveries made on their territories. The mayor of Neuvy-en-Sullias sent a message to Orléans, and the prefect lost no time in sending Paul Mantellier to the scene.

There are some who believe that archaeology is a newly born science, and that research carried out during the last century was wanting in efficiency. Now Paul Mantellier acted in the best way he could; he was a provincial scholar, but cannot be enough praised. He immediately took the necessary steps to protect the treasure, negotiated for it to appear in a public collection and began an important work for publication. Even though written a century ago, it is still of great value, and is the only study ever to have been made on the famous bronzes.

On June 1st, four days after the discovery, Mantellier was on the scene. The objects had been transported to the town hall and arranged haphazardly in the greatest disorder. The director of the Museum of the district of Orléans at once compiled an inventory of the treasure and placed it under legal protection. It was feared that certain objects had already been stolen; one of the quarry-workers could have kept some for himself. The mayor and priest of Neuvy-en-Sullias lived in fear of a robbery, and wondered where the treasure would be safe. The shutters of the town hall did not provide sufficient protection. So everything was stored in the very bedroom of the school teacher, who would sleep next to the rare bronzes. A few days after P. Mantellier's visit, they were seen by another local scholar, M. Pillon. He was authorized to enter the room, as though it were a sanctuary. The bronze horse was placed in front of the fireplace, its mantelpiece overloaded with objects.

M. Pillon was especially intrigued by the horse. "It is the same size as a wooden horse on one of today's merry-go-round," he reported. "It seems to whinny when the school teacher of Neuvy puts the bit between its teeth and shakes its bridle." Then the commentary becomes that of a connoisseur. "Its general appearance is that of a dray horse with a powerful neck and a small lean head. High of rump and low in the withers, it has short strong legs and muscular haunches and shoulders and, although light-footed, it has wide hooves. Our old Celtic breed has in no way degenerated."

The good M. Pillon, apparently a horseman, had nothing but praise. But in speaking of the other treasure objects, his attitude became indignant. He showered sarcasm on a statuette of a nude woman, holding up her hair. "This is so unbelievably ugly ... It is frightening." As for Mantellier, he used similarly pejorative terms; he considered the statuettes to be "mediocre art and of barbaric workmanship . . .. They belong to a period of complete decadence." 30 years later, the famous archaeologist Salomon Reinach did not mince his words either, and spoke of an "atrocious style" and of "specimens of Gallic realism in all their hideousness." Nevertheless, he recognized that this was "the most important discovery of works of art in bronze ever to be made in Gaul."

Whatever reservations there may have been as to the artistic quality of these objects, everything was done to prevent the dispersion of the treasure and to display it in the historical museum of the district of Orléans. The workers who had discovered it had a legal right to a part of it. At once,

Mantellier began negotiations with them, and they were lengthy and delicate. The land owner too could claim a part, but he generously conceded it. The total price was fixed at 7,045 francs, not a little sum in those days. So money had to be raised. The town of Orléans granted the museum board a supplementary allowance of 3,600 francs, and the local administration of the Loiret awarded a fund. On June 1st, 1862, exactly a year after Mantellier's visit, the bronzes were put in the Historical Museum of the district of Orléans.

An assortment of religious offerings

The treasure of Neuvy-en-Sullias consists of 32 objects, which are truly disparate in subject, dimensions and composition.

First of all, there is a group of 7 animals: the great horse, 3 boars—and fragments believed to be of 2 others—, an animal of the bovine family, a bull and a stag. Then there are 3 representations of gods: Mars, a Bacchic Eros and Aesculapius. Finally, there are 8 human statuettes, 4 women and 4 men.

The series ends with various objects: hanging-rails, an "umbo"—the central boss of a shield—and a trumpet—a "tuba"—4 feet 10 inches long, which is a very rare piece.

Some of these objects are in the pure tradition of Greco-Roman art and it is possible that they were imported. Others, on the other hand, are

certainly of indigenous origin; they evoke the
region well and are of interest for more than one
reason. They are worth describing here.

It is of note that the material that was dug up
is in bronze, smelted, beaten or indented. This
is curious. In such a collection, one would expect
to find iron, if not silver. But there is only bronze.

What is more, the discovery included objects
that had been discarded, rejects when they were
buried. We know this because the places where
they are broken bear a patina of age. There are
parts which are burnt, manifestly the victims of
a fire. They were undoubtedly sacred and were
not to be moved about; they had to be preserved
as if intact. It is clear then that the treasure was not
put away because of its intrinsic value—that is,
the weight of the metal—, but because it was a
religious deposit which had, at all cost, to be kept
away from the impious.

The evidence seems to show that the treasure
of Neuvy-en-Sullias is the deposit of a Gallo-
Roman sanctuary, and this will be dealt with
later on. The disparity of many objects, which have
nothing religious about them, could give rise to
objection. Perhaps the presence of animals is surprising. But, as will be seen, these probably have a
sacred nature based on the ancient Gallic tradition. Also, it should not be forgotten that offerings
of all kinds were accumulated in ancient temples,
and they were not only highly unpredictable but
also often preposterous. As an ancient writer
pointed out, they were not made "for the worship

and honor of god, but for the satisfaction and the vanity of men." Surely the same thing is true to-day, when jewels are heaped up at the feet of ven-erated Madonnas, like the Virgin of Guadeloupe?

One may well wonder what a "tuba" is doing in this collection. This is a trumpet. It is often mentioned in the ancient texts, and is known to have had an important role in Greece and Rome, but only a few very rare examples have survived to this day. One is kept at the Etruscan Museum of the Vatican; another, found long ago at Saint-Just-sur-Dive, near Saumur, is in the museum of that town; and there is one, found at Neuvy-en-Sullias, which is particularly handsome and intact, as only the bell is partly destroyed: it is 4 feet 9½ inches in total length, and consists of several sections of hammered bronze which are fitted together with forged bronze sheaths.

Perhaps this trumpet was a military instru-ment, for it is known that Roman troops were provided with them. Even in those days, military music existed. It is possible that a veteran offered it to the gods, just as today sanctuaries of Christian pilgrimages are adorned with sabres, medals or souvenirs of war, bequeathed by veteran soldiers. This hypothesis is supported by the fact that the treasure includes another military object, the "umbo" of a shield.

It is, however, generally preferred to attribute a religious nature to the "tuba" of Neuvy-en-Sullias. For there is considerable evidence of the role played in religious ceremonies. After the beginning of the 5th century B.C., the lustration of sacred trumpets took place twice a year. One may imagine, therefore, processions accompanied by the loud music of the "tuba" in Roman Gaul.

Was the god Rudiobus a horse-god?

Let us now look at the horse which is the largest bronze of the treasure, and also which has continuously attracted attention since its discovery. It is of hammered bronze and is no less than 3 feet 6 inches and weighs as much as 121 lb. 154 with the pedestal.

The beast is walking, with the left leg raised. The representation could not be simpler or better executed. The tail is something of a disgrace, but it can be seen that it was remade long ago, before the interment. The removable mane is carefully groomed and forms a kind of tuft above the head. The horse champs at a bit attached to the bridle which rests on the neck.

The photograph reproduced in this book renders a detailed commentary needless. But it is worth dwelling on the pedestal which, curiously, has a big ring at each corner. On the front, there is an inscription which has been the subject of much debate.

AVG. RVDIOBO SACRVM
CVR CASSICIATE DSPD
SER ESVMAGIVS. SACROVIR. SER IOMAGLIVS, SEVERVS

The first line is a dedication to the god, whose name is designated. The second contains the dedication: D.S.P.D. "De sua pecunia dedicavit," that is "has offered from his own purse"; and the third is about those who were charged with carrying out the offering.

None of this is very clear. The god is called Rudiobus; he is qualified as is fitting, as being "august", that is "venerable" or "holy". But it is perplexing that it is the first and only time that this name appears. No other mention of it was ever made in all the land of Gaul.

The second line also remains something of a mystery. What does CUR mean? Could it be the abreviation of "curator", that is, "right-hand man", "curator" or the abbreviation of a first name, such as Curius or Curtius? As for "Cassi-ciate", it is tempting to interpret it as the designation of a place which could be identified as a village near Neuvy-en-Sullias, today called le Chassis. Otherwise, this could refer to Chécy, a village about 12 miles from Neuvy.

As for the names of those who were charged with executing the offering, it is very interesting to note that they are of Gallic origin, though Latinized. Sacrovir has a famous homonym in the history of Gaul: Julius Sacrovir, the noble Eduan who revolted against Rome during Tiberius' rule, captured Autun, and was unwise enough to engage in a pitched battle against the legions, but was defeated.

It is hoped that the reader is interested in this

short gloss on the inscription. It is indicative of the problems of interpretation inherent in such texts, and the results are hardly satisfying.

To return to Rudiobus, this name is intriguing because, as mentioned above, this is the only time it has appeared in Gaul. It should be added to the already long list of Gallic gods. Some had their origin in the old Celtic culture, others were imported from Greece and Rome. The most important question is whether the famous bronze horse is an image of this god, or whether it was an offering to the god Rudiobus, who would then have had a completely different appearance.

I agree with the highly qualified specialists who believe that Rudiobus was a horse-god. For the big rings fixed to the corner of the pedestal could well have had shafts passed through them, enabling the image of the god to be carried and displayed at shoulder height during processions.

The pantheon of Gaul is full of animal worship. To continue with the horse, it appears with disturbing frequency on Gallic coins. Our Gallic ancestors had a strong aversion to the eating of horse meat, and this could be indicative of the worship of this animal. One should remember the importance given to Epona, that wholly Gallic divinity who had no equivalent in Greece or Rome. Generally represented riding side-saddle on a mare, she was the patroness of horsemen, travelers and all those who used the horse. It is quite understandable that this animal should hold a special place of honor among an essentially warlike and farming people, as were the Gauls.

It has been supposed that the horse at Neuvy-en-Sullias was saddled, but there has been no evidence to confirm this, although it does have the bearing of a mounted beast. In any case, it was not a free horse, which can be seen by the camber of the neck, the flared nostrils and the restive mouth champing at the bit. From this composition seems to emanate an expression of pride, as well as a spectacular style, effected by the tuft of mane crowning the head like a plume.

Sacred stags and boars

The stag, which has an important place in the treasure of Neuvy-en-Sullias, is known to have been an object of very special worship among the Gauls. There is much evidence of this.

There are many examples of Gallic sculptures representing a god adorned with antlers. His name is believed to have been Cernunnos. He appears on the cauldron of Gundestrup, a famous work of art which is in the Museum of Copenhagen, and in France he can be seen notably on the famous bas-relief of the "nautes" of Paris. This was found in the chancel of Notre-Dame, and is now displayed in the great hall of Gallo-Roman baths in the Museum of Cluny.

Although there has been much debate on this, we may say with caution that the stag held a manifold religious significance for our Gallic ancestors. That is to say, he was as much an infernal god as one of fertility, and at the same time the symbol of rebirth, because the horns grow back each year. Perhaps this evinces even a belief in immortality. It is astonishing that this cult, which had been predominant for several centuries before Christ, should have survived under the Roman occupation—the pillar of the "nautes" is an example—, and for a considerable time to come when Christianity was in full force. This is shown by the legend of St. Hubert.

There were three statues of boars in the treasure, and this was also a sacred animal of the Gauls. There is nothing surprising about the veneration given to this animal, the symbol of strength and vigor, as well as fury. These were qualities which were extolled among warlike peoples.

All these bronzes from Neuvy-en-Sullias were made during the Gallo-Roman period, even though no one has yet been able to date them precisely. That the horse should be of the 2nd century is but an hypothesis. Old religions dating from independent times were perpetuated even when Rome had full power, but she never tried to suppress them. It is questionable whether she could have. Rome was already so burdened with gods of all kinds that she had little reason to hold them all to account. The Gallic gods had a rough existence, and the Gallic character, whether in religion, politics or customs, never ceased to shine through.

Mysterious human figurines

The human figurines in the treasure, however, are much more difficult to interpret. The two most famous ones are reproduced in this book. It is interesting that they are all nude. One wonders what the running man represents, and the woman with the right arm outstretched, holding her abundant hair with the left.

One may try in vain to endow them with names of gods and goddesses. There is, however, nothing about them that permits us to attribute them to any divine paradise, so it is as well to relegate them to the more realistic world of mountebanks and dancers. The running man, who has thick curly hair and a trim beard maybe said to be holding a rope or a hoop. Perhaps he is a juggler or an acrobat. On his right leg there is a stamped inscription which is not very legible—perhaps SOVTO or SOLITO—and which teaches us nothing. The women with long hair are often, though gratuitously, considered to be dancers.

It would be simpler to regard these small bronzes, which are only from 3 to 9¹/₂ inches tall, purely as "sujets de genre" and as works of art without any particular meaning. An artist, or maybe several artists, gave free rein to their imagination and, for once, rejected the repertoire of Apollos, Herculeses and Venuses. One should consider these statues only from an artistic angle, and this is perhaps why they have been in disdain for so long. The qualifications heaped on them by

the good Paul Mantellier and Salomon Reinach
should be remembered here—"It is frightening . . .". But today justice has been done to them.
They were displayed in an exhibition in Paris in
1954 and they created a sensation. They were
likened to Bourdelle and other sculptors too, and
certain modern artists found in them a kind of
justification for their own work, and saw them as
remote precursors. For works of the past are
subject to judgments in which the prejudices and
fashions of today play a great part.

It remains to be said that these statuettes
reveal an extraordinary virtuosity, and an unequalled ease and mastery. This is art of a most
polished kind which obtains its effect by the
deliberate exaggeration of certain shapes, the
rejection of conventional disciplines and a supreme elegance of gesture and movement. That
which some may call clumsiness or naivety is, on
the contrary, a deliberate attempt at boldness.

It would be desirable to date these objects,
but that is not possible. As mentioned above, the
horse is generally believed to be of the 2nd century, and some would like the human statuettes
to be older. In any case, it is certain that these
objects were made after the Roman occupation.
The Gallic artists devoted themselves earlier to
purely decorative and stylized art, except in the
south-east regions which yielded notably the
famous sculptures of Entremont and Roque-
pertuse. One may well ask whether the objects of
Neuvy-en-Sullias may truly be considered to be

of Gallic origin. The answer is in the affirmative because their very inspiration was drawn from the worship of animal divinities, and also a distinct and blossoming art found full freedom to affirm itself, and to differentiate itself completely from Roman influences. It was, of course, after the example of Rome that the Gallic sculptors attempted to represent, in volume and form, human beings and animals. But they asserted their own genius, original temperament and personal style.

These statuettes of Neuvy-en-Sullias are very far-removed from Roman art. One should avoid thinking that the latter miraculously came into being at the stroke of a magic wand throughout the Roman empire, and that it spread in a disciplined and uniform manner. Admittedly, there were "provincialisms", but that is quite another matter. The important thing is that there existed true national arts, if one is permitted to use that word, and that of Gaul was one of the most original and assertive. The bronzes of Neuvy-en-Sullias bear witness to this.

An aura of mystery

In nearing the close of this chapter, the reader may have noticed that many questions have been reluctantly deferred. How mysterious the treasure of Neuvy-en-Sullias is!

Granted that the treasure belonged to a temple, we still do not know which one. It may

have been consecrated to the enigmatic Rudiobus, or perhaps he was only a "gues" in a
sanctuary consecrated to another god. As to the
location of the temple, maybe it was near the
scene of the discovery. This is a plausible theory
but remains unproven, in spite of the temptation
to identify "Cassiciate" with nearby Chassis in the
district of Neuvy. It is quite possible that this
sanctuary was at some distance, at least on the
opposite bank of the Loire, and that it had been
desirable to protect it behind the barrier, illusory
as it was, formed by the river.

As to when this hasty burial took place, the
period of the great invasions is usually suggested,
especially those which occurred at the end of
the 3rd century, and which caused great terror
throughout Gaul. One may also suggest a brutal
attack by Christians converted at Orléans at an
early date, who would have been anxious to
destroy pagan temples and religions.

The perpetuation of the Gallic tradition is
astonishing, as seen in the names included in the
inscription to Rudiobus, and in the sacred animals
fashioned in bronze. This district around Orléans
could have been a kind of "conservatorium" of
old traditions. It is tempting, at this point, to recall
the well-known passage of the "De Bello gallico",
Caesar said that "every year they (the Druids)
gathered together on a certain day in the land of
the Carnutes, considered to be the center of Gaul,
in a secret place." Now Neuvy-en-Sullias is on
Carnute territory, although this does not neces-

Statuette of man running. Height 8 in.
Photo Y. Guillemaut

Statuette of lady dancer. Height 5½ in.
Photo J. Suquet

sarily mean that the great druid gatherings took place in this village. It has been claimed that they took place in the forest of Orléans, and magnificent remains still exist on the north bank of the Loire, opposite Neuvy-en-Sullias. It is possible that sacred memories lingered on in the vicinity of this forest, and that cults which had a deep-rooted origin in Gallic religion were continued there.

The treasure of Neuvy-en-Sullias, then, is surrounded by an aura of mystery, which has not been dispersed for a hundred years, and probably never will be. But surely it is the privilege of beautiful works of art to cast fantastic veils of mystery.

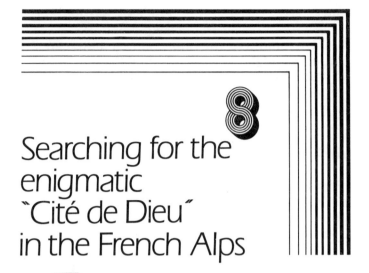

Searching for the enigmatic `Cité de Dieu` in the French Alps

East of Sisteron, in the Lower Alps, a winding road climbs the mountain. It is the *"Départementale 3"* which only leads to a few poor villages. To take this road you have to be an ardent lover of beautiful landscapes and solitude. After seven miles of a rugged ascent, it passes down through a narrow gorge, called *"Pierre-Ecrite"* (Inscribed-Stone), dominated by high limestone cliffs. There is just enough room for the road and the chaotic course of a small torrent.

Here, an enormous broken-off rock juts out skirting the road. It bears an ancient inscription composed of twenty majestically written lines whose letters have barely weathered with time.

What a uniquely moving contrast between the imposing austerity of the scenery, where the pale jagged stones reign, and this mark of man engraved into the rock which has traversed the centuries almost intact!

An enormous inscription on the mountain

It is not worth your time to try to decipher the entire inscription. The specialists themselves have come across difficulties in doing so, and it has provided subject matter for many discussions. In the first line you can easily read a name, that of Claudius Postumus Dardanos, and in the sixth line another name which, to say the least, is unusual to find here—*Theopolis,* the *"Cité de Dieu"* (City of God).

We learn from the text that it was Dardanos himself who had hewn into the rocks the route leading to his own domain. He had the latter encircled with high thick walls equipped with entrances, and he gave it the name of *Theopolis.*

The long inscription of the *Pierre-Ecrite* gives a flattering list of the titles that Dardanos, who lived from the end of the fourth century to the beginning of the fifth, had accumulated. He was *vir inlustris* (for *illustris*) and *patrice*—which placed him at the top of the aristocracy. He held some very high State functions: governor of the province of Vienne, one of the richest and most important of Gaul, and prefect of the Praetorian

Guard of Gaul. He had also been magistrate of petitions and palace quaestor, responsibilities which placed him close to the emperor.

But Dardanos was not the only one mentioned in the inscription which associated with his memory, his wife, Nevia Galla, herself *clarissima et illustris femina,* and his brother Claudius Lepidus, who had held high positions in the imperial court and had governed the province of *Germanie Première.*

It happened as a strange destiny for a man who acquired a place of honor in "high society" at the close of the Empire to have withdrawn into this remote spot in the Alps that he baptized *"Cité de Dieu".* Was it a gesture of Christian humility (for as we will see, he was a Christian); or was it the lassitude of a great lord overwhelmed by honors, who no longer had a place in a world ravaged by the Barbarians? Perhaps it was both.

Before continuing, we must stop an instant to look at this name of Dardanos which instantly strikes anyone familar with antiquity. In fact, there is a Dardanos in mythology who holds a place of honor. He was born of the marriage of Zeus with Electra, one of the Pleiades, and was the founder of Troy (the "Dardanelles" are named after him). However, *Dardania* not only designates Troy but also the country of the Dardanians—that is, Macedonia, which now corresponds to the present territory of Bulgaria and Yugoslavia—where Rome had recruited many faithful soldiers and servants.

Had our Dardanos taken this name to create
a flattering genealogy by implying that he was

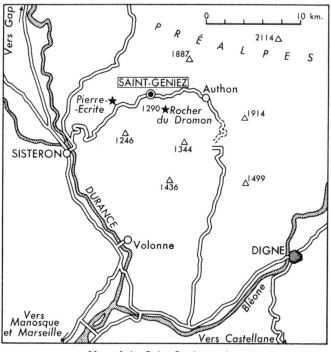

Map of the Saint-Geniez region.

a descendant of the founder of Troy? Or, does
his name reveal an Eastern European origin? It
had been a long time since the "pure" Roman had
become a myth. The imperial purple itself covered

Spanish, Gaulian, African, Pannonian, and Syrian shoulders. Rome had opened its doors to the provincials who often proved to be its best supporters. In any case, we can only hypothesize about the origins of Dardanus, prefect of the Praetorian Guard of Gaul. Some have wanted to attribute to him a Greek lineage and thus explain the toponomy of *Theopolis.* But one might just as well point to the true Greek snobbism that reigned at the end of the Roman Empire and for which there is so much evidence.

The last dark days of the Roman Empire

Contrary to custom, the inscription on the *Pierre-Ecrite* is not dated. No matter! Several texts provide information concerning historical passages and also two documents of capital importance, which will be discussed later: the letters written to Dardanos by Saint Jerome in 414, and by Saint Augustine three years later.

This is one of the most disastrous periods for the West—the final chaos of the Roman Empire. The immense edifice is attacked from all sides and is eaten away by the onslaught of the Barbarians. The decisive blow comes on the last day of 406. A "veritable invasion" (composed of Vandals and other Germanic peoples pushed to the west by the Huns who came from the far reaches of the steppes) crosses the Rhine, ravages *Germanie Première* of which Claudius Lepidus, the brother

The "Pierre-Ecrite" *inscription*

CL(AUDIUS) POSTUMUS DARDANUS, V(IR)
INL(USTRIS) ET PATRICIÆ DIGNITATIS, EX
CONSULARI PROVINCIÆ VIENNENSIS, EX
MAGISTRO   SCRINII   LIB(ELLORUM),   EX
QUÆST(ORE), EX PRÆF(ECTO) PRET(ORIO)
(*sic*) GALL(IARUM), ET NEVIA GALLA, CLAR
(ISSIMA) ET INL(USTRIS) FEM(INA), MATER
FAM(ILIAS) EIUS, LOCO CUI NOMEN THEO-
POLI EST VIARUM USUM, CÆSIS UTRIM-
QUE MONTIUM LATERIB(US) PRÆSTITE-
RUNT, MUROS ET PORTAS DEDERUNT,
QUOD IN AGRO PROPRIO CONSTITUTUM
TUETIONI   OMNIUM   VOLUERUNT   ESSE
COMMUNE, ADNITENTE ATIAN (*sic*) VIRO
INL(USTRI) COM(ITE) AC FRATRE MEMO-
RATI VIRI CL(AUDIO) LEPIDO, EX CONSU-
LARI GERMANIÆ PRIMÆ, EX MAG(ISTRO)
MEMOR(IÆ), EX COM(ITE) RERUM PRIVAT
(ARUM) UT ERGA OMNIUM SALUTEM EO-
RUM STUDIUM ET DEVOTIONIS PUBLICÆ
TITULUS POSSIT OSTENDI.

of Dardanos, is governor, and puts a part of Gaul to
fire and the sword. To evoke this devastating
onslaught, I need only quote this well-known page
from Saint Jerome:

"Countless, savage nations have succeeded in becoming the masters of Gaul. Everything between the Alps and the Pyrenees, the ocean and the Rhine had been devastated by the Quade, Vandal, Sarmatian, Alain, Gépide, Hérule, Saxon, Burgundian, Alemani and (oh what grief!) the Pannonians. It was really Ashur who came with them! Mainz, once a noble city, had been captured and destroyed, and thousands of men were massacred in the church. After a long siege, Worms had fallen. Reims, a powerful city, Arras, city of the Morins, at the frontiers of Gaul, Tournai, Speyer, Argentorate *(Strasbourg)*, had been transformed into Germania. Aquitaine, Novempopulania, Lyonnais, Narbonnais—all of these provinces have been devastated, with the exception of a small number of cities; and cities, which the foreign sword spared, had perished from internal famine."

A dismal communiqué, isn't it? How did the authorities react when confronted with this cataclysm? The government, the prefecture of Gaul, had retreated a few years beforehand. It withdrew from Trier which was too dangerous a seat, to take refuge in Arles. The fight between the aspirants to the imperial purple was merciless and each one recruited followers among the disarrayed populations who clung to the first arrivals who could show authority and act as the saviors. The *pronunciamientos* came one after the other and I don't intend to list them here. There were no less than five persons of rank claiming to be emperor when Alaric entered and sacked Rome in 410.

Among them, a Gallo-Roman named Jovian (not to be confused with the general from Reims who in the previous century had inflicted a crushing defeat on the Germains) taking command and relying on the Barbarians, was able to install himself in Trier which had already been overthrown.

But the emperor Honorius, who had retired at Ravenna where he vegetated amidst the palace intrigues, maintained the appearance of legitimacy and retained his followers. The outburst of Jovian was short-lived, for Dardanos attacked him and succeeded in separating the Visigoths, with whom he had attempted to make an alliance, from his camp. Jovian was besieged in Valence, captured and handed over to Dardanos at Narbonne, who killed him with his own hands. Those Gaulish nobles who had sided with Jovian were put to death. Honorius' power was momentarily restored.

In front of the *Pierre-Ecrite* inscription, one cannot refrain from recalling this dramatic scene: Dardanos killing Jovian, even though he was imprisoned, in the name of the law and justice of those in power. His behavior was badly judged by some of his contemporaries—above all, by Sidoine Apollinaire, one of the great and impetuous figures of young Christianity in Gaul, who became Bishop of Clermont-Ferrand and, in addition, left some poems in Latin, many of which are excellent.

Sidoine fulminated against Dardanos and made a monster out of him, so much so that his severe judgment endured a long time, blackening the memory of the former prefect of the Praetorian Guard of Gaul. During the Renaissance one can mention a striking detail: a great professor from Salamanca invented an adjective, *dardanarius*, as a synonym of vice incarnate.

Sidoine does not give any motives for his imprecation, but they can be explained not with religious but with political reasons. Had the Bishop of Clermont-Ferrand (who didn't know Dardanos since he was only born in 431 A.D.), reproached him for having mocked religion or for having personally executed Jovian? Not likely. It can be surmised that it was in reality Gaulian patriotism with an anti-Roman character which dictated his vehement position. In effect, Dardanos was the liege man of Honorius and to restore his rights, he sacrificed and put to death (as we have seen) the Gaulian nobles who rose up against the emperor of Ravenna. Of course later on, the latter was obliged to proclaim an amnesty, wiping the slate clean of the past. But, in the bottom of his heart, what hate must have remained! If at least Dardanos' repression had resulted in something positive! But no; it didn't stop the barbarians, and during his episcopate Sidoine Apollinaire had to undertake a ferocious struggle against them which led him to prison.

Moreover, one must put oneself back into the

setting of the first centuries and read, in this regard, the candid lines of Abbot Châtillon, who had studied Dardanos and his time in great detail: "All those great individuals who fill, from the beginning of the barbarian invasions until the Carolingian dynasty, the history of France and that one sees taking turns in either civilian, military or religious life, have found critics in the political field whose detraction has made them criminals, and admirers in the Church who have wanted to make them saints... At that time, the activities and abilities were not distinct and saintliness was no more a limited domain than intrigue or murder."

The correspondent of Saint Jerome and Saint Augustine

Even though the history of Dardanos is tainted by the violent denunciation of Sidoine Apollinaire, it is on the other hand exalted by two illustrious names, Saint Augustine and Saint Jerome.

For this man whose name is preserved on a rock in the Alps had been in correspondence with the two well-known Doctors of the Church. Moreover, they treated him like a great lord, in well-chosen, flattering terms. Saint Augustine called him *frater dilectissimus*—"very dear brother"— and Saint Jerome addressed him in this way: "The most noble of Christians, the most Christian of nobles, a perfect scholar...."

Dardanos, then withdrawn from the world, having taken refuge in his Theopolis, put to the two doctors some theological and exegetic questions—we would vulgarly say "stumpers"—and they answered him (Saint Jerome in 414 and Saint Augustine in 417) with letters that make up veritable treatises which, as such, have from their origin been judged worthy of being conserved and transmitted.

At that time, Saint Jerome was settled in Bethlehem where he founded a monastery near the grotto of the Nativity. He indulged himself in an intense literary activity, doing the work of an historian, a translator and as exegete to the point where, from his own acknowledgement, God reproached him in a vision for being "more Ciceronian than Christian."

As for Saint Augustine, he was Bishop at Hippo Regius during the time he corresponded with Dardanos, a position he had held since 396 and retained for thirty years, until his death. We know what the immense task of this prelate was. This untiring administrator, relentlessly fought the heresies of Donatism and Pelagianism which were especially threatening the Church in Africa. Nevertheless, he took the time to write to Dardanus. The reason was that even though this man had retired from public life, he was renowned and played an important role in the newly born Christianity. A pagan, had he just been converted? Or, already a Christian, had he decided to retreat to the high summits of spiritual life? Nobody knows.

The Roman Empire was collapsing in the West, but the reputation of Dardanos emerged from the chaos and crossed the seas.

In any case, it has been well proven that, though the extraordinary construction of Rome was crumbling physically, and though its frag-ments were lying on the ground as if an earthquake had scattered them about, close relations were sustained between men of quality whatever the distances that separated them and the events that opposed them. Through a de-caying world, spiritual ties formed a solid bond. Dardanos, who had retreated to an obscure place in the Alps, was in contact with Jerome in Palestine and Augustine in North Africa. And this was not just a temporary contact. It is evident that, no matter how far from Gaul, the two Doctors of the Church were following Dardanos' actions and conduct, aware of his position and knowing exactly how they should deal with him. The unity of the Roman universe, politically falling apart, was held together by Christianity.

From the Augustinian *"Cité de Dieu"* to the Alpine Theopolis

The eyes linger over the sixth line of the *Pierre-Ecrite* inscription where the name Theopolis stands out. It was to reach this place that the rock had been notched and that some hard work had been undertaken to open a passage for the road.

Unavoidably, a parallel must be drawn between the *"Cité de Dieu"* founded by Dardanos in the Alps and *The City of God,* which was the principal work of Saint Augustine.

Theopolis. This is, indeed, an unexpected name. It is a Greek toponym. What is it doing then in this remote spot in the Alps? Are there other names of this kind in Gaul? We have found two: on one hand there is Antipolis, which was a trading center founded on the Provençal sea coast in the fourth century B.C. by the Greek from Marseilles, and its name has been preserved in that of Antibes; on the other hand, there is Gratianopolis (Grenoble), a name which Cularo of the Allobroges took when the emperor Gratian, in 379, raised it to the rank of a city and endowed it with a bishopric.

Antipolis owes its name directly to its Greek founders, and Gratianopolis to the homage rendered to a sovereign, in a Hellenic style which was the custom in the Lower Empire. But how can one explain Theopolis other than by Dardanos' expressed wish to confirm his adherence to the work of Saint Augustine with whom he was corresponding?

Note that the famous *City of God* written by the Bishop of Hippo Regius, comprising a total of twenty-two books, was not completed until 426. But it began to appear thirteen years beforehand. From the beginning the title was in the air, and it wasn't long before it made its way to the Alps and was engraved in a rock. A marvelous progression of a thought, a striking witness to Augustine's eminence!

Now let us leave the *Pierre-Ecrite* and continue our ascent on the winding road. After several miles we arrive at Saint-Geniez, a little village composed of just a few houses. Here, the valley widens opening to form a circle, limited by the mountains which stand in a row, bathed in a limpid light. On the right, the Dromon, an enormous rock with steep sides, shoots up to an altitude of 4257 feet. Long ago, the summit could be reached by an old path which is now partly deteriorated. The ascent today calls for agility. It seems that at the summit of this extraordinary observatory, one finds two rooms cut out in the rock and the remains of massive walls which date back to the Middle Ages. One cannot help but admire the daring of these men who went up to the top to install a lookout post or a stronghold retreat.

A mysterious crypt in a humble chapel

The mind, haunted by the thought of Theopolis, would like to dwell on some kind of vestige, but nothing emerges from these green pastures or broken-up rocks. At the foot of the Dromon stands a large country cabin; outside, it resembles all those buildings used as barns and sheepfolds scattered about the Alpine valleys. It's a chapel, and only one path leads up to it. You arrive in front of a decrepit wall built recently to enclose a part of the edifice which had collapsed. Walk around, treading on the debris of tiles which lie on the ground; no apse projects from it; on one side, two bells sit on the ground, surviving evidence of a bell tower which has disappeared.

Turn the large key in the lock. The door opens with a crash, pushed by the wind which rushes in with you, as if, reigning in these premises, it won't dare leave you alone. You look around: the architecture, which was disfigured by re-building in the seventh century, holds no interest. There are several votive tablets, some rustic statuettes and some dried up flowers; you can see that very few pilgrimages still continue. Who are these rare individuals that come to this isolated place, and what graces do they seek? Are they not stirred by a sort of ancestral force, by a yearning due to a distant heritage and for reasons they cannot fathom? In these humble, secluded chapels, old religious practices are kept up unconcerned with ostentatiousness or moral compunction.

A winding staircase opens up in the choir. You walk down the steps in the dark and you find yourself in a little crypt that is confined and cramped. It isn't even twenty feet long, and has a very low vault. The rock shows through in many places, as part of it had been hollowed out. Consider the plan: the little apse has an apsidal to the left and right, which are not more than little cubbyholes, a tri-apse design.

There are four small columns with their backs

set into the walls of the crypt. Two of them still
have their capitals made of alabaster. One such
capital has a geometric design representing a
corbeil of entwined circles; the other is ornamented with rams' heads and two long tailed
peacocks. The juxtaposition of these kinds of
motifs is part of a very old Christian tradition and is
notably found in Byzantine capitals. Peacocks,
symbols of the Resurrection, are a frequent
theme used in Merovingian, Lombard and Visi-
gothic art.

Is this the mausoleum of Dardanos and Nevia Galla?

The date of these capitals in the Dromon crypt
is a subject for discussion. Some claim they go
back only to the twelfth century, but everything is
in favor of their being from the eighth or the
beginning of the 9th century. Even the plan of
the crypt, the tri-apse design that I mentioned
earlier, corroborates this early epoch. As the great
archaeologist Fernand Benoit has pointed out, this
is one of two very old Provençal constructions
dating from the Merovingian period: the Trinity
in the island of Lérins, and the Gayole (in the
vicinity of Brignoles) in the Var. The plan and
structure were adopted for the mausoleums
destined to shelter the bodies of venerated men.
    You see where I am leading: all evidence
suggests that this crypt had been constructed

several centuries after the death of Dardanos to honor this burial ground or to collect his venerable remains as relics.

An important point would be to know who the holy person was that initiated the practice of a pilgrimage to the little chapel. The oldest records, which go back to the eighteenth century, mention the liturgical feast of two Persian martyrs, Abdon and Senen. Later on, their commemoration seems to have disappeared, and the Feast of the Virgin Mary replaced it. Furthermore, the dates of the pilgrimages don't coincide with those of the feasts and one wonders if it was just simply an agricultural feast that was celebrated at the Dromon chapel, a solstice rite like the other examples found in old French sanctuaries.

As can be seen, little is known about this pilgrimage which, as I have shown, seems to have had varied purposes with the passage of time. Nonetheless, the site has been venerated since a very early time, for some coins have been found there from Constantine's era. Fernand Benoit, who has studied the mysteries of Dromon, thinks that the cult could have sprung up because of the possession of relics pertaining to Dardanos and his wife Nevia Galla, ranked as saints for their example of Christian virtues and their search for asceticism, so highly regarded during the first centuries.

Upon entering this little crypt, so silent and somber, memories of Dardanos and his wife Galla are irresistibly evoked. One would certainly like to have the proof that they were buried there. A few years ago some hasty diggins were done, but they need to be taken up again with a more persevering method—especially on the north side of the Dromon chapel. There, on a lower level, remains a small apse, the fragments of an adjoining chapel, which is in the midst of a chaos of stones and debris. This must all be cleared away to arrive at the rock on which it stands.

A "so-called place"...

However, in admitting that this little Dromon chapel had originally been a *martyrium* where venerated bodies were kept—perhaps Dardanos'—the mystery still remains. Where was Theopolis?

First of all, let's not let our imagination run away, thinking that a real city could have been built in this Alpine lap. The *Pierre-Ecrite* inscription tells us that the road cut out of the rocks leads "to a place called Theopolis." How should one interpret the word "place"? This can be quibbled about endlessly. In any case, the inscription speaks of large walls and doors. Furthermore, the significant road work that was carried out implies that Theopolis, while not a city, was nevertheless a large dwelling. Immediately one thinks about one of those great domains, one of those *"villas"* which were flourishing in Gaul, notably at the end of the Empire, when troubled times provoked a desertion of the cities and a movement back to the land.

The villa was a domain supported by the land, consisting of the master's house, farm buildings and some basic industries. It could include several hundred people, organised, as we would say today, in an autarky. It was, in a way, the ancestor of the village.

That is what Theopolis must have been: a vast agricultural domain living from a few crops, fruit trees, livestock, timber production and also the nearby mineral resources. In effect, to the south of the Dromon rock the Vanson valley begins. Here, next to a tributary of the Durance, pyrites, silvery lead and anthracite, were mined. Naturally the proximity of the combustible material to the ores gave birth to a little metallurgic industry which must have gone back to ancient times.

The *Pierre-Ecrite* inscription explicitly mentions that Dardanos established Theopolis on his very own land *(in agro proprio)*. We can believe that he owes this land to his wife, Nevia Galla, who must have been a Gallo-Roman (though, as we have already seen, he was himself most likely of Oriental origin), that he probably knew at the time of his nomination as a high official in Gaul.

Hence, one can well imagine what happened. Dardanos held the highest official functions of the empire. Faithful to Honorius, he suppressed with brutality the *putsches*. To what good? His action didn't stop the collapse. Rome was besieged by Alaric's hordes. Disillusioned, tired of his functions and worldly honors, yet strengthened by the faith, he decided to retire to his domain. The place is frozen in the winter, scarcely productive, but its remoteness offers a double advantage: it is sufficiently secluded and clear of the large roads to escape the barbarian attacks that beset Gaul; and secondly, its seclusion, along with the beautiful and sweeping scenery, favors and inspires religious life.

This was truly to be one of God's domains, Theopolis. The inhabitants were to form a Christian community under the strict direction of Dardanos. The former high official, who had been the friend of emperors, must have manifested some disdain towards the well-known bishops and pastors of the region. Had he come up against a moral dilemma? Did he want to clear up some doctrinal point? He addressed himself, across the seas, directly to Saint Jerome and Saint Augustine. And from the latter, he even borrowed the name, "*Cité de Dieu*" (City of God).

Will we one day rediscover the lost city?

How we would like to find some kind of vestige of Dardanos' Theopolis! If you go there, you will search about these rocks and pastures, places which, alas, remain implacably silent. You will linger on the level areas, thinking that they were able to support settlements. You will scrutinize the differences of level, closely examine the slightest little rock and pick up the most insignificant debris. Your quest will remain hopelessly vain.

There have been others before you who have tried to make the land speak. Some have wanted to associate the name of Theopolis with that of Theous, an out of the way farm difficult to reach. Others have thought that the *"Cité de Dieu"* could have been erected on the terrace called *"Les Planeaux"*. More likely, one can guess that Theopolis was situated in the locality of the village of Saint-Geniez and of the Dromon chapel. The distance between the two is one and a half miles. You can see that it's a vast area on which one could undertake research.

In any case, one should take a closer look at Saint-Geniez. In fact, the village was named after *Genesius* (a town clerk beheaded for having refused to transcribe an edict of persecution of the Christians), a saint particularly venerated in the church at Arles, precisely where Dardanos was positioned as the prefect of the Praetorian Guard of Gaul. At that time, wouldn't Dardanos have expressed a special devotion for this saint, and wouldn't the name of the little village date back to this time?

But all of that is mere supposition and vain hypothesis. Excavating in the little Dromon chapel is being considered to see if Dardanos' sepulcher is underneath. Just the same, the question of Theopolis will not be resolved. Throughout the centuries, those living in the mountains have certainly salvaged the useful rocks. The foundations themselves could have disappeared in the violent mountain torrents that upset and wash away the earth in this region.

Besides, who told us that the *"Cité de Dieu"* consisted of neat large buildings? After having known courtly life and after having lived in palaces, Dardanos withdrew to an austere site with trying weather. Had he still been attached to worldly goods, to material advantages, he would have installed himself in a more hospitable region. The very fact that he retreated into the depths of the Alps, ready to brave all the hardship that that represents, proves that he had deliberately chosen the path of true asceticism. Thus, he had never intended to build a rich residence. Without a doubt he was content, as those with him who followed his example, to live in modest buildings made of roughly hewed rocks like the ones that can still be seen scattered about in the surrounding pastures. Perhaps Theopolis had only been a very large hermitage where Dardanos, his family and his followers—free men and serfs—lived an exemplary Christian life. Before continuing on the road, one lingers with a strong wind beating against the face in front of a circle framed by rough mountains where, long ago, Theopolis once stood. Nestled at the foot of the huge Dromon rock, the little chapel with its secret crypt gives a human dimension to this fierce landscape. How difficult it is to leave this place! The beauty, mystery and overwhelming past that dominate it

are captivating. It seems as though the powerful
voices of Saint Augustine and Saint Jerome echo
among the rocks.

The discovery of Rome's gigantic defensive structure on the Sahara's edge

t the beginning of the 5th century, the Roman Empire was no more than a senile white-haired man with his limbs falling off eaten away by leprosy, invaders that strike at every frontier. The head was sliced in two: one emperor ruled in the West, the other in the East. Rome was no longer even in Rome: the capital had been transferred to Ravenna.

Even though the imposing edifice was cracked and disintegrated after four centuries of grandeur, there remained some solid and faithful territories: Roman-Africa. It too had been shaken by serious upheavals: Gildon, a native leader whom Rome had imprudently made head of its troups, revolted; but a brutal repression reestablished order and the rebellion didn't see another day.

Surviving on the other side of the Mediterranean Sea, this Roman power was based on two pillars: the landed aristocracy and the Catholic Church. Both of them amply benefitted from Roman order; and the structure of the society they maintained out of concern for their own interests rather than any deep attachment.

The Church in particular formed a solid and powerful organization based on 600 bishoprics (at the same time Gaul only had 100). These were often led by great individuals of whom the most illustrious is Saint Augustine. At the same time, the church still held real political power and worldly riches. On the religious level, it had to stand up to a redoutable schism: Donatism. To eliminate it, just as to maintain its privileges, the Church needed Rome's assistance.

And above all, Rome could not survive without Africa for providing food and supplies. The Empire was being eaten away, losing numerous territories that helped provide its sustenance. As it was split in two, Constantinople took for itself the provisions furnished by Egypt. Africa had to send its products to Rome—its wheat, oils, wines, horses, not to mention its heavy taxes. What hurt Italy the most in Gildon's revolt was that the chief rebel had stopped the shipments of wheat. The invaders pressed from all sides, but if they could only have eaten their fill . . ..

A text from the Theodosian Code

Now, on April 29, 409, the two allied emperors, Honorius and Theodosius II (a quite ludicrous character called Calligraph because he had a mania for beautiful writings) sent a message from Ravenna, to Gaudentius, their vicar, that is their prefect in Africa. Here is the text, which is included in the Theodosian Code. The entire text is given because all of the terms deserve to be weighed and will reappear throughout this chapter like a leitmotiv.

We have learned that land granted to some gentiles *(associates) by the foresight of the ancients, with the purpose of assuring the maintenance and the protection of the* limes *and the* fossatum *were sometimes occupied by plain citizens. If these latter satisfy their greedy aspirations in occupying this land, let them know well that they have to devote their loyal services to the maintenance of the* fossatum *and to the manning of the* limes, *like those that the ancients have appointed to this function. If this condition is not filled, let them know that the most elementary justice will be to transfer these concessions to some* gentiles, *if one can find some; or at least assuredly to some veterans in order that, these precautions continuing to be observed, one can not fear the least danger in any part of the* fossatum *and the* limes.

Written at Ravenna the III of the calenders of May under the consulate of Honorius and Theodosius II.

What does this text mean? That the emperors of Ravenna had one major preoccupation to, at all costs, maintain the *limes*—that is, the defensive structure which protected North Africa as far as the Sahara. Did rebellious peoples from the south threaten to invade and to devastate the Roman territories? Perhaps. But above all, the African *limes* was the only frontier in the Empire which was not yet overrun by barbarian hordes. For the emperors, overpowered on all sides, the maintenance of the *fossatum* and the mounting of a guard at the *limes* were essential tasks. First of all, note the distinction made in the imperial text between *limes* and *fossatum* : we will come back to these later on in the chapter.

The emperors addressed their representative Gaudentius in a manner which we find surprising and even moving. They gave orders, but with self-control, as though they were not quite sure of their being carried out. And on two occasions, they appealed to the providence of their forefathers. This reminder of past times, of the 'golden era' is rather sad . . ..

The zenith of Roman power and glory was, indeed, truly past, and almost forgotten amid the misfortunes of time. The year, as I said, was 409. For five years, Rome had been abandoned in favor of Ravenna and, a year later, the capital would be invaded and ravaged by Alaric and his hordes of Visigoths. The message to Gaudentius from the emperors was dated in April. In the autumn of the same year, the Vandals who stormed Gaul were to reach the Pyrenees. This was just the first stage in the migration which was to lead them to North Africa. Invasion from the south was feared; the *limes* and the *fossatum* were to be outflanked. It was from the west, to the hordes come via the Strait of Gibraltar, that Roman-Africa fell. In Chapter XII, I will describe the Vandal Empire as it existed beyond the Mediterranean Sea.

From the Air Force to archaeology

The *limes*? We knew what this defensive structure was that the Romans had used to surround their Empire. But the African *limes* and *fossatum* remained a mystery. There could be no doubt of the latter's existence, the Theodosian Code supported this, but there was no evidence of it to be found on the site. It remained an enigma, a word devoid of meaning ... many people judged that *limes* and *fossatum* referred to one and the same thing.

However, at the beginning of the century, we were close to discovering something new. In fact, for a long time some ruins were clearly discernable in the earth, sixteen miles south of Biskra, which the inhabitants of the region regarded as those of an enormous *seguia*, that is an irrigation canal. It was thought that in the past it had been dug in order to draw water from the Wadi Djedi, a Saharan river which was usually dry, but which frequently produced diluvial torrents, that were expended spreading through the vast area formed by the Chott Melrhir. The volume of these ruins was such that they were surrounded by a legend, that of a queen, named Bent-el-Krass, who in the distant past had this marvelous construction built. The officers in charge of regional affairs had surveyed this so-called *seguia* and the great archaeologist Stéphane Gsell had the remarkable foresight to see in it what he called the "trench of Roman frontiers"—both *limes* and *fossatum.*

However, the mystery of the *fossatum* remained intact. The imperative letter from the emperors was in fact addressed to the curate of Africa, as if the whole of Africa was jeopardized, while it was really only a question of a local section of "border-line trench" (which was, moreover, attributed to a much earlier era). The mystery was finally to be cleared up in 1947, thanks to a sensational discovery, by a colonel in the Air Force: Jean Baradez. The airplane came to the aid of archaeology. From the sky, the earth was obliged to reveal its secrets.

In 1945, Jean Baradez, who had been promoted to colonel, reached the age limit for flight personnel—which for a colonel/pilot is forty-seven years of age. He was like an albatross fallen to the deck, but a new career was open to him to which he would from then on devote his tireless activity: specialist and innovator of 'avant-garde' aerial observation, he adapted this technique to archaeology. An enormous field was open to him; he was to exploit it masterfully. In a few months' time,

Excavations in London. A team of archaeologists free a group of sculptures.
Keystone

Head, thought to be Minerva, in marble. It is believed to have had a crown of br
Photo Guildhall Museum

he was able to announce that he had discovered the renowned African *fossatum*, an essential part of a *limes*, very different from what had been imagined.

Of course Jean Baradez didn't claim to be the founder of aerial observation applied to archaeology. Notably, before him, there was, between the wars, Father Poidebard's remarkable research in the Syrian desert. Although the revolution of archaeological processes of investigation is slow, aviation in general and aerial research in particular have since made great progress. In Algeria, a land so rich in history and with such a wealth or ruins, the archaeological work carried out by French specialists is considerable, but the airplane has as yet only rarely and very sporadically been used for exploration.

Jean Baradez used only existing pictures taken for a specific purpose which were as far removed from archaeology as possible—pictures which have already passed through many hands, which have been used exhaustively and which were filed away without having revealed the archaeological secrets they contained.

A great archaeological discovery from some pictures intended for dam construction

Now the department in charge of hydraulics and colonization in the General Algerian government had made a 'spread' of 120 negatives taken, at an altitude of 13,000 feet, a few years previously to study a project for a dam at the spot known as the 'Fountain of the Gazelles'. This site is relatively near the El Kantara Canyon, one of the greatest natural sights in Algeria; gorges with impressive walls, entirely red and at the bottom, carpeted with palm trees, which towards the nearby palm-grove of Biskra form a majestic gateway to the desert.

Jean Baradez spent many long days studying the negatives. From them he recorded all the archaeological remains on a map which he drew up as he went along: Roman roads, towers and small forts, *castella* and innumerable anonymous traces left by man in zones which today resemble the steppes or semidesert regions.

It was already a great success. But then he noticed a thin furrow, ever present in the reliefs, He followed it on different pictures. Could it by any chance be the *fossatum*? At first he hesitated; if in actual fact it was the construction in question, it was situated sixty-two miles north of the only section already located by that time: that of the *"seguia"* Bent-el-Krass, and in a general direction perpendicular to it; in addition, no trace had ever been pointed out by anyone. But he was soon forced to believe that it really was the *fossatum*, with an amazing volume of both principal and secondary defense works. We 'possessed' a new section, about eight miles long. But we had yet to understand its vital mechanisms.

We cannot overemphasize the vital point that the revealing pictures had not been specifically taken for this purpose; they already existed. The whole problem was to know how to read and interpret them. Imagine a manuscript filed on a shelf of archives. Contained within are pages of history, but it will remain lost to the world unless it is confided to a specialist. It is the same for an aerial photograph; it gives a picture of the earth as it exists and appears today, but more important it can reveal the land's history. Obviously, not just anybody can discover these secrets; the buried history is only revealed by details, sometimes seemingly unimportant. The color of the earth, differences in vegetation, minor movements or erosions of the earth only show up under certain lights. And so there are scars engraved in the earth, traces of human works which, in a specialist's eyes, are like sudden glimpses of the past. But above all, in Baradez's own particular method of analysis they are "captured humidity stains" which not only uncover constructions hidden by the relief, but allow us to 'see' and detect these constructions or their remains which are completely hidden under the perfectly level surface of the ground.

Jean Baradez was familiar with the methods of military interpretation of pictures, of which he was an innovator, but he also applied to archaeology all that he had used and perfected during twenty-five years of service: locating installations, defense works, enemy camouflage and, most important of all, beyond the identified structures which revealed material complexes, turning prob-

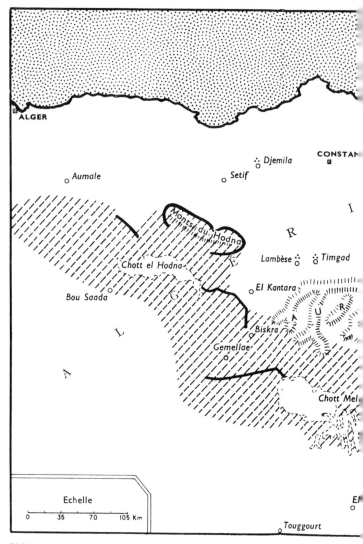

NORTH AFRICA AND THE "FOSSATUM"

It was impossible to give here a detailed map of the limes and the
fossatum which stretch over considerable distances. The location of
the limes is marked by shaded areas. As for the fossatum, the main
sections known have been marked by a heavy line.
Only a precise description of the reliefs would allow understanding of
the steps taken by the Roman engineers, particularly in order to link
the system over the mountainous chains and the chotts of the South.

In fact, the geography determined the layout of the barrier, whose purpose was basically to block all possible invasion routes.

The scale of our map has not allowed us to show the numerous castella, large and small forts, built progressively over the years along the fossatum, nor those which helped to "link" to their network the successive components of the limes.

Note the special configuration of the system around the Hodna Massif. It must have surrounded a "patch" of dissenters contained in these rugged mountains, and it is almost certain that it belongs to a plan devised at least two hundred years later than Hadrian's limes.

lems upside down, referring back to the source, deducing the determinate concepts and the enemies intentions in order to draw far-reaching conclusions.

He was to study the Roman *fossatum* as he had studied the Siegfried line or the positions in the campaign in 1940 when he was in charge of reconnaissance on the Maginot line: he would take apart all the machinery, he would reassemble in its entirety. He would "put himself in the shoes" of the producers and substitute himself for them in his mind to understand each apparent anomaly.

An immense human work in an inhuman landscape

As this *fossatum* was revealed in this manner on aerial pictures, the question comes to mind: how was it that it had never been spotted on the ground? But here lies the real magic of aerial detection by a specialist. In making your way across the expanses traversed by the trench, you will see no sign of it: this is a kingdom of shapeless stones, the desolation of the steppes and the desert. The ancient construction, enormous as it was, has been completely destroyed.

Once the first results were obtained, Jean Baradez received an official mission from the General Algerian government. I will not undertake to now retrace the stages of the discoveries which followed in rapid succession. The *fossatum* grew:

twenty-five more miles by 1947, sixty-two more by 1948. Soon the colossal work of the Romans would stretch over more than 420 miles.

By 1949 Jean Baradez was in a position to publish an extensive work entitled *Fossatum Africae—Aerial Research on the Organisation of Saharan Borders in the Roman Era.*

But it is time for me to explain the composition of the *fossatum.* It is without doubt a simple trench, as its name indicates, but this is not all: we will show that it was, on the contrary, a very complete and fairly complex passive barrier.

Do not imagine that today we can see this trench running across the desolate plains, un-folding like a wide band. In these areas subjected to the extremes of nature, burning sun, excep-tional differences in temperature, wind which nothing can stop, infrequent but brutal tornados, the work of man corrodes and is wiped out quickly. As I said earlier, Jean Baradez often had difficulty actually finding the trench after having spotted it by airplane. One day, an Algerian who accom-panied him in his wanderings made this vivid observation: "This thing which crosses our country and which we learned of through you, what is it? It's like the wake of a boat on the sea."

Excavations have, in any case, allowed us to reconstruct its profile. It was a triangular shape of different dimensions around ten feet deep, from three to ten feet wide at the bottom and ten to sixteen feet on the surface. Lovers of math could measure the cubic volume of earth excavated over a distance of several hundred miles. Truly, the Romans produced prodigious earthworks. One can imagine the mens' efforts, digging and shovelling, fighting against rubble... The excavated earth was added as an extra obstacle to the trench to make it as effective as possible. Behind, a few feet from the trench, a large wall was built with dry stones, often constructed of huge blocks, into which the towers were incorporated.

In the mountainous zone, the trench did not follow the more or less linear layout of the flat Saharan section: it used the lay of the land in a remarkable way, and as a rule followed the steepest slopes where the waves of enemies were slowed down and left open to blows from the defenders. Here we must forget our modern conception of well-defined frontiers marked by posts; under Rome, the land was divided to the best advantage; it was the right of the conqueror. The Roman engineers who marked out the route of the *fossatum* had no political contingency to take into account; before them stretched the barbarian world—vast lands on which there were no settled peoples, but only nomads wandering around in thinly scattered groups. You may raise the objection that such a trench was not, after all, an impassable obstacle. Doubtless this is true, but as I said earlier, the *fossatum* was not just a large trench and a wall, a ditch and ramparts. The passive obstacle was in a way "brought to life" by the defenders who, and Jean Baradez has

proved this, never had more than a half-hour walk
to their combat posts from the villages where they
lived, the existence of which was unknown until
these searches were made.

Here and there, and at least at each change
of slope and direction, were huge towers with
extensive views, reinforced by other larger
towers, allowing visual communication with the
side or supporting constructions. Further back, a
second parallel route doubled its strength, notably
allowing the rapid intervention of auxiliary troops,
flanks of cavalry or cohorts of mounted infantry.

This then was the system of the African *"fossatum"*, quite simple, in fact, but effective. It was
hardly any different, in reality, from the system
used for the other "ditches" in the Empire, particularly the one which blocked the north of England—about which I shall speak later on. This kind
of set-up required constant maintenance for the
trench filled in with landslides; the wall and
towers in dry stone were not very sturdy. This is
why, in the spring of the year 409, an appeal
given by Ravenna reached the borders of the
desert: "Look after the *fossatum*!"

This obstacle was, moreover, only a stalling
line which formed the last element of a very
complicated system. Further to the front in the
vast zones where mobile units patrolled, where
nomadic peoples lived more or less under the
control of the Romans, small forts rose up, surveillance and alarm towers, and sometimes larger
constructions.

The *fossatum* proper covered, on the contrary, virtually all of the vast area which had been cultivated using extraordinary water systems and, as I will point out later, the country folk who had settled on the conquered land of the steppes took arms in case of an alarm and occupied the *fossatum.*

Fortifications and roads

The forts and supporting constructions for a great part ran along the *limes,* of which the *fossatum* was the backbone. Some of them were very large. One example among so many others which Jean Baradez discovered is the huge *castellum* situated to the north-west of Biskra, approximately halfway between this oasis and the Chott el-Hodna, and which he calls the Grand Fort of Zebaret. Built in a rectangle, it measures no less than 505 feet by 466 feet surrounded by a wide trench; it had only one gateway protected by two square towers. Towers and bastions are in the corners and along the walls. The defense was powerful. In the center of the courtyard of the fort, there was a *praetorium*, quite square, with sides 133 feet or so long, numerous rooms to lodge the troops and shops. As far as we can gather, this construction even included public baths nearby.

It was believed for a long time that the African *limes* was quite a trivial defensive structure, basically meant to guard against the *rezzous* of the nomads. The discoveries made by Jean Baradez prove that it formed—within the limits of the ancient cultivated land, but today in the Sahara—a real Maginot line.

A military highway, this *limes* was linked to a very dense network of roads: the secondary route to the *fossatum*, roads leading to the interior, roads parallel to the border and roads meeting and crossing at oblique angles. Everything was provided for the rapid intervention by the defenders, brought in like troops from interior garrisons and for promptly displacing them from one spot to another on the *limes.* On this level too, Jean Baradez, thanks to his research on aerial pictures, was able to masterfully complete our knowledge. On paper, he reconstructed the majority of the Roman roads, and the cross-checks on the ground which he made with the help of local excavations later on proved the accuracy of his observations. This was how the identification of a road to the west of El Kantara, which was completely invisible on the ground and moreover hardly distinguishable on the aerial negatives, was to lead to an important discovery: that of twenty-two milestones grouped over a distance of only three Roman miles.

We know that Roman roads were marked by milestones erected at the time of building, or rebuilding. They constitute precious sources of information because they mark not only the distances, but also the name and title of the reigning emperor, and they reveal periods of activity and in what field the activity was directed.

The milestones which Jean Baradez found at the site, some of which were still standing, doubtlessly formed the richest harvest which had ever been made in this branch. One extraordinary thing, was that they lay almost on the surface only a few hundred yards from a trail, and they had remained undiscovered. There were twelve at the X mile, five at the XI, and five more at the XII. They were spaced out from the beginning of the third century until the end of the fourth, and represented an extraordinary list of emperors—some of them famous, others transitory or of no special interest: Elagabal, Alexander Severus, Gordian, Diocletian, Constance Chlore, Licinius, Galerus, Constantine the Great, Constance II, Constantine III, Gratian, and even more. The sound of these names, rising out of the sands, eloquently brought to mind the contrast and stubborn efforts used by Roman power to keep their roads in good condition.

Louis Leschi, director of the antiquities of Algeria, could not resist coming to the site to see such a discovery. On that day, the hint of scepticism which he showed at the beginning in regard to the rather revolutionary methods employed by Jean Baradez completely disappeared . . . . He then began to edit the preface of the latter's work. "This book," he recorded, "marks a step forward, perhaps the most decisive one so far, in research into the past of North Africa."

The *limes*: a border zone

While the *fossatum* had just been discovered in its entirety, the *limes* too appeared, in the course of the research, to be very different from what was until then imagined. It was no more a linear border than the *fossatum* was the trench border accepted until then. The depth of the Roman plan was however revealed day by day, and Jean Baradez could give a new definition of a *limes,* which, moreover, applied to all the borders in the Roman Empire.

To simplify matters, one could almost translate *limes* exactly by "border zone". In Roman-Africa, such a zone stretched out in depth over vast areas. Travel over them today: stripped barren they are the realm of bad weather, the "country of intolerable splendour" spoken of by André Gide, who wandered so readily in the area of Biskra which the ancient Roman *limes* crosses. At first sight, one can hardly believe that numerous peoples could have lived there in ancient days, attached to the land—today so desolate—which they had to defend. It is one point in Jean Baradez's favor to have shown how this zone was developed by the Romans. The former student of the National Agronomical Institute became passionately fond of agrarian archaeology. He was able to analyse the huge structure over which the Roman engineers of rural engineering presided, that is, the specialists of the Third Legion. His study of agricultural water systems is as exciting as his military and administrative studies which won for its author the Grand Gold Medal from the Agricultural Academy in 1951.

Is the contrast between the present poverty of the land and its past prosperity due to a change in climate? Not at all, although it was once claimed to be so in a rather simplified way. A historian, a contemporary of Hadrian is very precise; the first rain for five years fell when the emperor made his second journey to Africa in 128. This made him very popular with the Africans who claimed that he had the *baraka* as they say nowadays in the language of the barren regions.

The ancient prosperity was indeed due to the immense labours carried out to protect the earth from erosion and to hold back—in the gigantic sponge-like belt of land hemmed in by an incredible network of walls—the seasonal waters, so spectacular and so brutal, in order to direct them, now more settled, towards the places where they were to be used often several miles away.

This work of giants was not carried out on simple individual initiative; it necessitated an overall plan, carefully studied and carried out with strict discipline. The land under cultivation had been chosen discerningly. That of the palm-grove was limited because, however profitable it might be, it is a prodigious drinker of water; the olive trees and cereals balanced each other out, the mills and grindstones which have remained in areas which are now arid bring the surprising evidence of this ancient agriculture snatched from the desert, organized and looked after by prodigious human labor.

Settled in this still living land were *'limitanei'* who served the Empire as farmers cum soldiers. They were like those Israeli settlers from the kibbutz near the Arabian border who work the land, guns slung across their backs. And in Algeria itself, didn't Marshall Bugeaud make settlers of the soldiers who stood ready to take up arms?

These *limitanei* were made up of a very peculiar cross-section of peasant life. Some were former soldiers, coming from regular units or auxiliary troops; others were natives, called up and kept permanently in contact with Roman authority through the arid land, whose water system constructed by them had assured their survival. By defending the *limes*, everyone defended their own possessions, their fields and their cultivation. The only danger of the system is that, attached as they were to the land, there was the risk of their putting down roots. As Jean Baradez said "from being soldiers cum farmers, they became farmers cum soldiers". Their presence alone would not have been sufficient for the defense of the border zone. They needed additional help, some dynamic troops always ready to make rapid interventions.

Unless strict discipline in matters of hydraulics and agriculture was maintained, the *limes* were neither fit for human life nor even defendable. It all had to be looked after with the greatest of care and run with faultless discipline. The day when Roman power flagged, the admirable organization fell apart and, little by little, the prosperous areas reverted to the steppes and the desert. What a sad picture this zone of *limes* is today, despite efforts employed by the French administration to bring back life to certain places! Jean Baradez noted: ..."What frightening contrast between the traces of what used to be and the appearance of what remains!... The area is horribly devastated nowadays by deep ravines which develop and branch out everywhere where the Roman protective works have not held. The desolation is even more haunting here than in the Sahara itself... In these huge areas, baked by the sun, only broken up and marked by very rare showers and whose wind sweeps over the disintegrated elements, there are no more inhabitants."

A town of the Saharan Ys: Gemellae

What discoveries about the zone of *limes* were made by the study of aerial pictures! Not only the *fossatum* and all the defensive structures of the *limes* were revealed but also the roads, agricultural water systems, and inhabited areas. Among the latter, Jean Baradez discovered and excavated a real town: Gemellae. Situated eighteen miles as the crow flies to the southwest of Biskra, it was not spotted on the group of pictures made for the study of the Fountain of the Gazelles Dam, but during the flights made by Jean Baradez.

Two of the large plates among the Augst treasure when they were discovered.
Photo Professor Laur-Belart

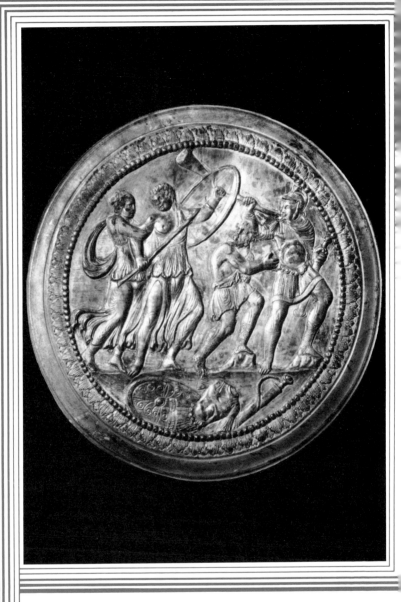

Augst treasure. The central medallion of the large plate of Achilles, sign
Pausylypos of Thessalonica. *Photo Professor Laur-Belart*

This followed his first discoveries which enabled him to understand the most minor details and articulations of such a defensive system whose volume was, to begin with, completely inexplicable in desert regions.

Gemellae was renowned for its inscriptions. It is known that it had the advantage of being a colony under Latin law, and also that it was the seat of one of the command positions of the *limes*. But, misguided by false toponomy (the oasis of Mlili came from Gemellae, so it was thought) archaeologists remained perplexed by its possible location.

The desert city of Ys—it seemed that it was to remain buried forever. But now it was betrayed by the swelling of the land, indiscernible on the ground but perfectly visible from the sky. Jean Baradez made out its plan and ramparts, gateways, monuments, roads, amphitheatre, dwellings and temples. What could be more touching than the shroud of sands opening to deliver the secrets of the dead town. In the center was a large military camp of rectangular shape, and all around it an inhabited area of imposing size which in one particular era, extended far beyond the limits of the surrounding well and the *vallum,* which were, however, 6,560 feet long.

Jean Baradez then started the exploration of the dead city that he had unwittingly unearthed. These were the first excavations that he undertook. Up until then the past had been revealed to him from overhead, but now he came to grips with the earth and forced it to surrender its remains.

He concentrated his research particularly on the great military camp around which the urban center had been built. The camp was encircled by its own wall which included a wide double moat and a defensive wall ten feet thick into which towers were incorporated; in the middle rose the *praetorium*, the center of command for the fortified zone of the *limes gemellensis*. Its ruins were buried under several feet of sand. What were they going to find? Jean Baradez, putting his heart and soul into the work, was uneasy. The workers were not long in digging up pieces of ruined architecture and also some inscriptions.

An obliterated inscription illustrates a page of history

One of these inscriptions was enormous, ten feet long, and it held the place of honor on the portico of the *praetorium*. It carried a dedication by the *Legio III Augusta* to the emperor Hadrian. The name of the legion had been obliterated, and then rather clumsily restored later.

One can hardly think of Roman Africa without including this Third Legion. A unit traditionally attached to the guard of a great part of the territories beyond the Mediterranean Sea—Tripolitania, Tunisia, all of east Algeria—it was really, with the attached auxiliary units, the "African army" familiar with the country and its people,

with which it had many ties. Its unity and its
discipline, shown during peace-time as well as
during war, was exemplary but, at the beginning
of the third century, it was severely punished and
broken up.

Let me outline the main facts of a dark page in
Rome's history, for it is illustrated by the monumental inscription at Gemellae. At the end of the
Severes dynasty, the Empire's future was truly
uncertain; it was open to the whims of some and
the audacities of others. One day, revolution broke
out in Africa due to heavy taxes. In 238 the rioters
proclaimed the African pro-consul, Gordian—who
was an old man—emperor. He could hardly hold
on to his power although he was recognized by the
Roman Senate and several provinces, and did not
reign even three weeks. The Third Legion did not
recognize him; it confronted the militia that he had
called up and they, without experience in combat,
did not last long before the professional army.

The old Gordian and his son, whom he had
forced to join him, were killed. In the same year,
two emperors succeeded him and were both killed
in turn. The events happened in rapid succession,
with bloody consequences. Before the end of the
year 238, Gordian III, old Gordian's grandson,
donned the imperial robes. The first thing he did
was to avenge himself on the Third Legion which
had killed his grandfather; he broke it up and
dispersed its soldiers among the Rhetian units and
in the regions around the Danube. Even its
memory had to disappear; its name was obliter-

ated from all the inscriptions in which it was
mentioned.

But the anarchy didn't stop and fifteen years
later the former soldiers of the Third Legion
dispersed on the Upper Rhine offered their
support to a new candidate for the Empire;
Valerian. Once in power, he restored the old unit,
which took up its former posts. Its name was re-
engraved on the inscriptions from which it had
been rubbed out.

An inscription lying in the sand at Gemellae,
with a name which had been obliterated and then
restored, is all that is needed to bring to life
important pages of Roman history. Such is the
character of archaeology as it reinforces history
and illustrates it . . ..

But this inscription, which evokes so many
historical images, was not the only one to be
discovered in the ground at Gemellae. In the
center of the *praetorium*, still erect beneath ten
feet of sand, stood an altar raised on two steps; the
altar to military discipline—the very same before
which the legionnaires took their oath. A plinth,
the statue has unfortunately disappeared, carried
a dedication to the Emperor Hadrian by the *Cohors
prima* of Chalcis in Syria, proving that the Roman
army was indeed installed on the Wadi Djedi one
hundred years earlier than was originally thought.
Opposite this, a statue had been erected in honour
of the Emperor Pertinax—who had, however, only
reigned ninety-seven days, at the end of the
second century, by the *Ala I Pannoriorum* (Panno-

nia stretched from the Danube to Illyria). Further away, in a small temple outside the camp, an altar had been consecrated to the protective gods of the camps by the *Ala Pia Fidelis* of Thrace and another by the prefect of the Pannonian flanks.

Thus, out of sand rose up the ghosts of all those soldiers who came from the far corners of Europe and Asia to guard the desert in the name of Rome. Some were infantry and others cavalry; they formed a sort of foreign legion, always ready for a fight, willingly posted in very unwelcoming garrisons and in posts lost in the wilderness. And it is in a place like Gemellae that one realizes how extraordinary the architecture of this Roman world was, everything being ill-matched and different, and yet so strongly cemented.

A Second century Vauban: the Emperor Hadrian

But there is one question to be answered: at which date was this great structure, the Roman *limes*, built? Actually, it is difficult to establish the chronological order. In the early days of Roman presence, the conception of the Roman *limes* was exciting and dynamic; and the Great Trajan, emperor from 98 to 117, had maintained a frontier policy of military movement and activity and of territorial expansion. With the coming of Hadrian, who was his successor and reigned from 117 to 138, there was a complete turnabout: he introduced settlement and stability to the front lines of defense. There is no doubt that the creation of the African *fossatum* in its first form, as well as the implantation of peoples who were responsible for the defense in the area of *limes*, were his doing. This, in any case, is the conclusion that Jean Baradez reached at the end of his long and definitive studies; the foreign specialists in the study of the Roman frontiers are in full agreement with it.

A wise and peaceful Hadrian had had a brillant past in the army: he had been in command in Germania and had waged war in Dacia; and, once in power, he decided to stop the conquests, to fix the frontiers, and to limit the military effort which was too expensive for the empire. In Germania, he gave form to and reinforced the *limes*. In England, between the Tyne and the Solway Firth, he had a strong wall built against the troublesome peoples of the north. Traveling throughout the Empire, wishing to see for himself the steps to be taken, he came to Africa in 122, where he made a second journey six years later.

It was during the second journey that he inspected the Third Legion at Lambese, where he reviewed the troops of the African army and made a long speech to them. Lambese, near the present-day Batna, not far from the Aures, whose mountains are outlined in the background, has conserved some magnificent ruins of its *prae-torium* and, faced with this important monument, our thoughts turn to the memory of the emperor and the ostentation of the review which took place in this location, still so impressive after so many centuries.

Less fortunate than Lambese, Gemellae has completely disappeared. It is true that, situated much further to the south, it was built in the Saharan style like the large buildings that can still be seen nowadays in the desert oases. Foundations of stone, white-washed walls of unbaked bricks—all this looked very nice but it could not withstand the test of time. The building of Gemellae dates from two years before that of the great camp of Lambese. We can suppose that the decision to erect these two camps were taken at the same time. The construction of Gemellae, the large command station of the *limes*, was completed more rapidly as its architecture was of a simpler style. As for the camp at Lambese, the seat of the procurator, henceforth the base camp of the Third Legion, it was a part of the prestige policy, the aim of which was to assert the power of Rome against the difficult people of the Aures.

But let us get back to the *fossatum*. Everything points to the fact that the decision was taken by Hadrian; it is in keeping with his thinking and his general policy. But many constructions, additions or transformations have later been grafted onto this framework according to the ideas and the needs of the moment, according to the dangers which threatened and the means at hand to ward them off. In the diverse constructions gradually erected on the *limes*, the traces of Gordian III,

Diocletian, Constantine and many others besides, may be found. Certain places were even reoccupied by the Byzantine reconquest after the tragic period of the Vandals.

The initial layout so well studied by the Roman engineers, so well suited to the possibilities of the land would always keep its tactical value. In this connection, Jean Baradez had a very characteristic adventure. One day he was doing a survey from an airplane of the *fossatum* in south Tunisia towards the Gulf of Gabes. Thick dust was clouding the atmosphere and hindering his search when he was surprised to see a beautiful trench clearly engraved in the ground, paralleled by another, the latter being nearly obliterated. At first, he thought he had found a particularly well-preserved part of the *fossatum*. It was in fact an anti-tank ditch dug by Rommel during the last world war to bar possible access to Gabes. It was almost adjacent to the ancient ditch. A *bunker* had even been installed on top of the obliterated remains of a Roman work. What a compliment to the Roman engineers choice after so many centuries!

The work done by Hadrian was to last three centuries. The farmers cum soldiers whose job it was to guard the *limes* carried out the mission with which they had been entrusted. Then, with the central power dwindling and becoming corrupt, discipline relaxed at the frontiers. For this reason, the order given from Ravenna by Theodosius II and Honorius is like the pathetic call of a crumbling empire.

The obsession with the desert

One remark probably comes to mind: this *limes* and this *fossatum* constituted a fantastic construction, but were they justified? Did the peoples of the south represent such a danger?

Obviously, one is tempted to think that the threat seemed worse than it really was. Of course, the Sahara has never had enough resources to enable an invading army to assemble there. But there was the menace of *rezzous*, of those lightning attacks which have always been peculiar to the Saharans. To stop them, a fool-proof device was needed. Could one have asked the regular troops to do it? One might as well have asked Rome to renounce its claim to North Africa. Remember that the desert guard was to stretch an immeasurable length, from Morocco to Egypt, practically from the Atlantic to the Red Sea. All the legions of Rome would not have been enough. The only solution was the *limes*, an organization with depth, at certain points breaking into the unconquered or simply protected regions, with sentry posts and a barrier—the *fossatum*.

The Third Legion whose task it was to defend a large part of North Africa hardly numbered 5,000 to 6,000 men, all of them infantry except for a small group of cavalry. On top of these there were a few thousand auxiliaries who made up the flanks of the cavalry or cohorts of the infantry. One can see, that all in all, it was a bare minimum force. Moreover, the army in Africa like all the other

Roman troops did not only have military tasks: it was responsible for a large part of the road networks and for the country's facilities.

The heavy obsession of the Sahara, expanses of unknown lands, gripped the Romans like all the other inhabitants of North Africa. Remember France's slow progress in the Sahara, the consternation caused by the massacre of the Flatters Mission at the end of the last century and the period of contemplation which followed.

This troubled anxiety that the Sahara inspired was not simply paranoia on the part of the Romans; they felt the reality of the "Moorish peril". Many times they had to struggle against the raids and pillaging of the Saharan nomads. In the time of Tiberius, a Berber who had served in the Roman army, Tacfarinas, rose up against the Roman power; he united groups of nomads and wanderers, stirred up a large part of the south and it took at least seven years to put an end to it all.

The Romans even had to lead some daring raids across the Sahara. We have records in some texts of three of these distant expeditions: one led by Cornelius Balbus in 19 B.C., one led by Septimus Flaccus in 70 A.D., and one led by Julius Maternus sixteen years later. For the first one, Pliny has given us an itinerary as well as some names; we cannot identify them today but certain authors think that Cornelius Balbus was able to push a small force as far as Hoggar. In any case, the Third Legion had a permanent detachment at *Cidamus*

—the present day Ghudamis—a little place deep in the heart of the Sahara.

The fear of the plundering Saharan nomads was such that whenever they were captured their punishment was harsh and exemplary. They were brought into the towns to be punished in the open in front of the crowd. One mosaic in Zliten, in Libya, shows two "barbarians"—Garamentians who occupied the Fezzan—chained to chariots and left to be torn to pieces by wild beasts.

But we must be careful not to consider the African *limes* and its *fossatum* as being structures peculiar to this continent. They are only parts of the gigantic chessboard set up along the length of the borders of the Empire on Hadrian's orders.

In Africa, they "marked the limits" of the land transformed into wheat fields and olive-groves by the emperors' agricultural policy. They were traced like the *vallum* in Britain was itself traced between the Scottish moors, mist-covered lands and the agricultural zones; like the *limes* of Germania was traced, for its part, to the east of the rich plain lying between the Neckar and the Rhine.

Briefly summarized these are the discoveries and conclusions of Jean Baradez. They throw much light on the pages of Roman history which had, until then, remained in obscurity. At the outset, their author had undertaken a survey of a defense system—the *fossatum*—which led to an immense study of the politics, the administration and even the Roman civilization. Archaeology is often like that: through the material facts that it reveals, the intentions and works of men can be reconstructed.

In addition, Jean Baradez proved by a large-scale experiment which he has, moreover, greatly developed since—the unrivaled contribution that the patient and methodical interpretation of aerial photographs can bring to archaeological knowledge. Photographs no longer, as in the beginning, concentrate on a few particular points but make up part of huge "spreads" taken at great altitude and covering thousands of square miles. Is it not a paradox of our time, but how satisfying, to see the most modern means used in the research and discovery of the most ancient times?

Discovery of the "Vandal Tablets" on the border between Algeria and Tunisia

 sad year's end for the Roman Empire which struggled in the throes of deprivation—December 31, 406—the day the hordes crossed the Rhine, undoubtedly frozen solid, near Mainz. Three sections were Germanic and the Vandals made up the majority. A fourth section, the Alains, came from a far-off land, the Caucasus or Iran.

Uno fumavit Gallia tota rogo: "All Gaul burned like a torch." This terrible and true statement is from a witness of his times, the poet Orentius. Three years later when nothing remained to ravage, the invaders passed into Spain. Would they finally settle down? Not at all. In 429, the

Vandals reached North Africa. Did Roman traitors provide them with a fleet? Possibly. Numbering 80,000, they succeeded in crossing the Strait of Gibraltar, pell-mell—women, children and slaves. Warriors? They must not have been more than 12 or 15,000. At their head was a very great king, Genseric. In a few months they had sacked all of North Africa. Saint Augustine took refuge in Hippo, now Bone, and died during the siege.

Vandalism, a recent word...

Decidedly these Vandals, savage destroyers, deserved to give their name to vandalism which, according to the classical definition, is "the state of mind which leads to destruction of works of art and beautiful things." What is less well known is that this word is a modern creation. The French Academy, always prudent, did not officially accept it until 1835. It had been invented by the notorious Grégoire, constitutional bishop of Blois, in a report to the National Convention in which he denounced "this vandalism which knows only destruction." It must be believed that the creation of this word corresponded to a need since it rapidly met with immense success and Grégoire could flatter himself by saying that it was "instantly naturalized into all civilized European languages." One reaction, quite unexpected, became evident; in Germany (where the word had to be adopted in turn) this pejorative reference to the Vandals was badly received. The "insult to their forefathers" was protested beyond the Rhine, and Schiller retorted that the real Vandals were the French who brought Grecian marble to the banks of the Seine. Words sometimes have curious fates . . .

But let us return to North Africa. It was under the Vandals for a century, less one year, from 435 until 534, at which time the Byzantines expelled the Germanic invaders. It would be erroneous to think that all of northern Africa was in Vandal hands. Their small numbers of warriors did not allow inordinate expansion. Their land was limited to a territory, quite large actually, roughly including Algeria east of Constantine, Tunisia, and a part of Tripolitania. After their wanderings the Germanic barbarians quite comfortably settled in the warm, fertile areas. This sunny land had an extraordinary attraction! Later, during the Middle Ages, the Crusaders would settle in the Near East, the Normans would relax and stay in Sicily and, nearby, the Hohenstaufen would forget their austere German cities . . .

After arriving like a tornado in North Africa, the Vandals rapidly grew wise. What better thing could they do—in their own interest—than to maintain, insofar as possible, the structure and staff of the Roman administration? The provinces continued to be ruled by governors and one of them was even led by a proconsul. The cities were governed by municipal administrations. The tax service regularly gathered revenues. Roman Law continued in force in all affairs where a Vandal was not concerned. Were the officials Romans? Not at all; they were Romanized Africans. They had changed masters and were satisfied by the trade. The important figures in the Roman administration had disappeared just like the big land owners. A raising of the level of the middle and lower classes resulted. Decolonization problems are not new ones...

What happened? The Vandals, taking advantage of their easy victory, lost their warrior's virtues; comfortably established on their great estates, they greatly enjoyed the profits. They tried to imitate the Romans and their taste for construction too. Thus Carthage was adorned with new monuments and games were revived there as during Rome's greatest days.

Fifty-six wooden tablets

This Vandal period, chaotic and uncertain, dominated by the "barbarians" who were not concerned with recording their history, is in fact not well known. As always, when written texts are rare, archaeology is called upon, but even this is desperately lacking in material.

Thirty years ago, however, an important discovery was to astound the specialists and give them some material for study which lasted several years and engendered long and scholarly dissertations. This happened in 1928 in the steppe regions which extend from the Algerian and Tunisian

One of the Vandal Tablets.
Photo Saint-Clair

Ruins of the industrial oil works at Brisgane which bear witness to the ar
prosperity of the vicinity of Tebessa. *Photo Marcel Bovis*

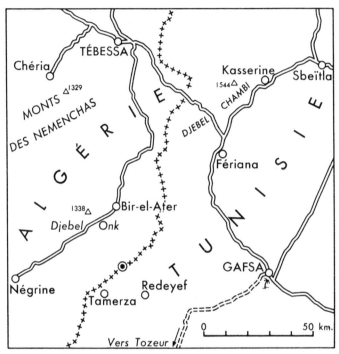

Map of the border between southern Algeria and southern Tunisia. The circled point on the border marks the approximate location of the discovery of the "Vandal Tablets".

borders to the northern part of the great Chotts. A secretary from the "mixed commune" (an administrative territory at that time) of Morsott, residing at Tebessa, was able to obtain five wooden tablets covered with curious inscriptions which the Moslems had found, it was said, in jars buried close to a wall. They were asked to continue their search. In all, fifty-six tablets were assembled.

The exact site of the discovery may never be known; according to several witnesses, it has been narrowed down to a zone located about sixty-two miles from Tebessa and forty miles west of the Tunisian city of Gafsa. These tablets were evidently not even found in the ground. One witness's report, which I just mentioned, would have it that the tablets, contained in jars, were uncovered by a flash flood which washed away the base of an ancient wall. According to another version, the tablets, hidden in a jar, came from a fortified rampart where they had been inserted in a dry rock wall. It was impossible to resolve this problem.

Eugène Albertini, who was the director of ancient Algerian artifacts at that time, learned of the discovery. He immediately realized its importance and hurried to make a first report on it that same year to the Academy of Literature and Inscriptions. The famous documents retain the name "Albertini Tablets". And this is justified, after all, because the great specialist from the very beginning established that they were documents from the Vandal period—while some thought they were Arab or even Hebrew. Moreover, he set out to classify the documents and decipher them. When he died, in 1941, he had obtained—after twelve years' work—interesting but still incomplete results. It became obvious that only a team could carry out the work undertaken.

Jérôme Carcopino entrusted this to Louis
Leschi who succeeded Eugène Albertini as the
director of Algerian artifacts, and to Christian
Courtois who was to prove himself to be a great
specialist of the period presaged by his memorable thesis on "The Vandals and Africa." These
two, before the magnitude and difficulty of the
task, joined with Charles Perrat, professor at the
Ecole des Chartes and Charles Saumagne, hon-
orary general secretary of the Tunisian government, specially entrusted with the legal problems
caused by the tablets. It was only in 1952, finally,
i.e., almost twenty-five years after the tablets were
discovered, that complete publication—thanks to
these four great specialists—put the finishing
touches on this research.

What are these tablets like? They are small
boards, more or less rectangular in shape. The
longest measures ten inches, and the widest, four
inches. The thicknesses vary from 3/32 to 3/8 of an
inch. The wood is half from cedars and half from
deciduous trees. The former did not exist in the
region where the documents were found and they
must have come from the Aures, a plateau with
magnificent forests at a distance of about ninety-
three miles.

The remarkable state of preservation of the
tablets is striking when their age is considered;
just a few changes caused by fungus and no
damage due to animal parasites. The reasons are
the extraordinary resistance of the cedar heart-
wood and, also, the odor of this wood which acts

as a disinfectant and anti-parasitic agent for the other wood which was enclosed in the same jar.

These tablets had been re-used often, after scraping, and under the most recent text, older texts appear—which does not in any way aid deciphering. The writing was done in ink with a pen undoubtedly carved from a reed. The ink? It does not seem to have contained mineral elements and it is thought that it was produced—as is still done today—from the basic ingredients of burnt wool and the dried fruit of the carob-tree, native to North Africa. In any case, after fifteen centuries it is still remarkably clear.

The reign of Gunthamund

What a magnificent windfall these little tablets of wood were, which crudely sprung (how, we don't exactly know) from the region all uncovered, radiant but meager. They formed the depositary or archives—the only one of its kind—upon which, as I said, the specialists zealously labored. There are so few documents from this Vandal period . . . It is an entire century of African history which remains hidden in darkness. You will say that this is not a singular case in the annals of history, but these hundred years attract and hold our interest in a special way. What an adventure it was for these hordes come from Germanic lands to build a kingdom beyond the Mediterranean Sea! Great names, like those of St. Augustine and Carthage, appear as its history unfolds in which the proud construction that was Roman Africa is finally eclipsed. And all this came to pass in a setting that present-day events have pushed to the forefront, and that excites our sensibilities. Even at that time the dangers from the Aures plateau that menaced the Vandal domination were not entirely eliminated.

But I have not yet told you what these famous tablets are. Certainly, they are not texts which tell of important events and royal gestures which would supply us from the start with great pages of history. They contain mainly sales records for real estate, grants made of certain parcels of land, made around the years 493 to 496 in a single region called *Tuletianos*. Each record normally contains the date (the year indicated is that of the reign of the Vandal lord at the time), the name of the seller, the object sold, the purchaser's name, the agreed price, the sales terms and the signatories (parties to the sale, witnesses and scribes).

You will say that, being so limited in purpose, these tablets arouse little interest. At first glance, maybe, but think of what the experts can extract from these documents: the language and writing used, the level of instruction, the nature and use of land and crops, their legal system, life-styles, organization in the country, the current prices, etc. Archaeology doesn't search for sensational finds any more, ornaments for museum exhibits. It sets great store by these documents which are in no way sensational, but allow the moments of everyday life to be set down and put man back into

his customary existence. The humanist archaeo -
ogy has replaced the esthetical—that of the work
of art.

At the head of the records appears the name of
the Vandal king of that period: Gunthamund,
called *dominus rex* or *dominus noster rex* and,
more rarely, *dominus invictissimus rex*. He was
the third Vandal king in Africa. His name probably
meant "He who protects the combat". Not much is
actually known about him. He did not have a very
vigorous personality and, also, he bore a heavy
patrimony, that of his two predecessors who stand
out; first, the notorious Genseric, who reigned for
fifty years and represented "an impressive combination of political virtues at least for someone
who does not look at things from the moral point
of view," to quote Christian Courtois; and,
secondly, Huneric of whom it can only be said that
"a bloody haze obscured half his reign." When
Gunthamund took the throne, the war-like spirit
that motivated the Vandals had diminished excep-
tionally in strength. The rough characteristics of
the race had been mollified by the contact with the
warm African lands. In general it is well known that
settling down brings an end to nomadic ten-
dencies.

In any case, during the reign of Gunthamund
pressure from the unconquered populations
began to heighten. Beforehand, the Romans had
had to build a virtual "China Wall" against them:
the *fossatum Africae*. As for the Vandals, they
couldn't even imagine this; they formed a single

warrior cast (and undoubtedly were not able to put more than 20 to 30,000 combatants in the field). At first, they had ensured their own safety by instigating a veritable terror, but constant intimidation is not a lasting governmental policy. The people of the Aures and the Nemenchas mountain folk, great nomads of the South, mounted dangerous raids to plunder the Vandal inhabitants. It was at that time that the Albertini tablets must have been buried. During dangerous times people tend to save records. Would the lands be ravaged? At least the titles would remain and be claimed once the hurricane has passed.

Where Rome survived under the barbarian yoke

The records in question are drafted in Latin. Within a framework of ready-made legal Latin, special notations have been inserted; this produced a rather curious mixture of official and normal languages. Louis Leschi, with the help of P.-J. Miniconi, demonstrated this conclusively but, nevertheless, we cannot conclude that it was an "African" Latin which was developed on the continent by combining the language of Rome with native tongues. It has been established that the writing on the tablets was done by thirty different people. It is a beautiful sampling which was studied zealously by specialists in deciphering ancient handwriting, paleographers, who were happy to have found, aside from papyrus, such an opportunity for studying the small letters of the fifth century—so close in principle and yet so far in its flowing forms from those of our typographers. In this area, the examination of the tablets was entrusted to one of the greatest masters we have on this subject, Charles Perrat, professor at the School for the study of Ancient Documents (Ecole des Chartes). It would be beyond the scope of this book to record at length all the observations and conclusions he made.

At most the records reveal the handwritings of simple country folk. Spelling errors abound and the syntax is badly managed. No matter! Documents like these which cry the truth, full of authenticity tinged with dirt, can have more value in the eyes of the specialist than the many Roman inscriptions whose perfection reflects the official character and which are written in a stilted style. The expression *"qui litteras nescit,"* "Such and such a person . . . illiterate" is often found, but it is, however, striking that, among these peasants who were so poor (we will later see just how low their level of development was), illiteracy was not more common than was actually the case. If certain ones needed the help of others to record their transactions, they at least knew how to sign their names. Anyone who has leafed through the ancient rural archives of our countries has seen the many x's which represent signatures . . . "Such and such a person, cannot read or write": this expression had certainly survived until quite recently . . .

What is the reason for the relatively high level of educational development in the Tuletianos region? Was there a small school in the area? Possibly. The role of the clergy can also be considered in North Africa where Christianity had become deeply rooted. The Vandals, who were Arians, obstinately resisted the Catholic clergy and hierarchy but were unable to drive them to the extreme limits of their kingdom. Thus one of the tablets mentions a *presbyter*, a priest named Saturninus.

As I said before, the bills of sale conform perfectly with Roman law. For three quarters of a century the Vandals reigned over this country and were unable (but did they really try?) to change the social structures and way of life, at least not in the back country. Obviously the unchanging character of the country, its conservatism, can be considered; but, in this case, there is something else. If the Roman framework persisted with this strength, it was because nothing had arrived to replace it. The Vandals had a military machine, and in contrast, a very weak legal system. Moreover, they were only a minority among the masses in which they were submerged.

Thus, from that time on, this phenomenon of "progressive fusion" occurred which has been noted in the history of great invasions, in Gaul as anywhere else. Once the plundering fleet has passed, the conquerors—few in number—melt into the conquered population which has the advantage of being more numerous and adapted

through the ages to the land and in general is of a
more refined cultural level. What would have
happened if the Vandals had not so zealously
clung to Arianism (this doctrine, as is known,
ended up denying Christ's divinity) which basically opposed them to African Christians. It was
this religious barrier which was largely responsible for their retaining their originality. If they
had not, they would have, sooner or later, been
absorbed by the masses they had conquered.

When a man and a tree have the same price

Thus, the Albertini Tablets proved that the
Tuletianos region retained, for a long time after
the Vandal immigration, the way of life which the
Roman Empire had imposed. What was it like?
Actually, quite poor. The level of life of these good
country folk has been evaluated. The price of an
olive tree, which constituted the principal revenue
source, varied from twenty to a hundred old
French francs (four to twenty cents—current
prices are a hundred times higher). Apparently,
the price of manufactured goods was considerable, almost out of the question. One of the most
interesting documents on this subject is one which
listed the dowry of a young fiancée, Geminia
Januarilla. She received a *dalmatic*, i.e., a large
tunic with long sleeves, which represented the
price of 125 olive trees. A veil used to cover the
head was worth twenty-five olive trees, a hand-

kerchief, nine, and a shoe, nine. A marriage on these terms bankrupted the parents . . .

The value of a person was barely as high as that of a fruit tree. Domitianus sold a small six-year-old slave named Fortinis to Germinius Felix. The price? A few cents in gold. This was very cheap and, also, the record specifies that Fortinis was a brave child with a good physique and was "neither a vagabond, of bad morals nor of fragile health."

Hence they had a very limited purchasing power—all these peasants, whose meager possessions were, nevertheless, in due and proper form recorded in the transactions. This gave a real solemnity to their records as if they concerned rich properties and, in any case, provided them with very strict guarantees.

Consequently, through the tablets we can see how these country folk lived, with their attachment for their meager possessions, with their distrust too, and their bargains. The names have been found of about 150 peasants in the Tuletianos region. For the most part, they could have been inhabitants of Latium or Narbonnaise. A certain number, however, seem to have retained beneath the latinization their African origins. Germanic influences brought in by the Vandals? They have not been revealed.

A description of life in a countryside which is today a desert

Naturally, the tablets give us much information on agriculture of that era. A curious thing: the records mention no cereals which, however, must have existed. They were undoubtedly considered supplementary crops grown beneath the fruit trees as we can still see today at oases in the Sahara. Indeed, these fruit trees constituted the basic wealth. The olive tree was the leader, followed by the fig tree. These two species are today—in the area in question—botanical curiosities, veritable residual flora.

So what has happened since the Vandal period? Take a tour of these vast, slightly rolling plains today which are cut by mountain chains extending from the massive Chotts. They are literally burnt, subjected to torturous changes of temperature (it has been observed that the temperature varies from 39° to 118° F.). Rain is sparse and the streams, normally dry. This is the area of esparto grass and wormwood, the desolate steppe countryside. A few bushes and parcels of cultivated land mark the expanses which, in their monotony, seem limitless.

Here and there, ruins, some of olive oil presses, recall the prosperity of yesteryear, and the Albertini Tablets confirm this. Have there been extensive climatic changes since the Vandal period? They could only have been very slight. Thus man must be accused. It is he who allowed the land to die. How? Mainly by abandoning the agricultural water system.

These famous tablets constantly mention wells, water courses and the networks of *seguias* to which title was transferred with that of the land they irrigated. The extraordinary importance of water in arid regions requires authority, discipline and a permanent collective effort. Digging and maintaining wells and canals, construction of retaining dams in ravines and maintenance of trees which prevent disastrous erosion, all this is the result of an organized State. The Roman Empire represented this framework and the Vandal domination preserved it to a certain extent, but decadence had already set in. Small groups of nomads, especially with herds of goats which greatly damage the land, settled into areas which were from then on not cultivated.

A short time later, the Great Arab Invasion completed this deterioration. This phenomenon is surely not peculiar to this section of Africa. This was established by the famous Colonel T.E. Lawrence in the Sin Desert when he was still engaged in archaeology. More recently, the admirable aerial observations made by Colonel Baradez, who discovered the *Fossatum Africae*, revealed what during Roman domination in the sub-desert regions of Eastern Algeria was the prodigious water works organization, which enabled people to live in the immense regions which are now the steppes.

Reading the records written on the Albertini

Tablets is for us a description of the life which surged from the depths of this now desolate country. Geographers could find a good subject for study in the changes in countrysides.

What lessons were contained in these tablets discovered one day in 1928! Very dark pages of history were brought to light but, to decipher and interpret them took long years of patience, research and, also, teamwork. Archaeology requires knowledge and utilization of very diversified disciplines. More and more it looks to various specialists who work collectively with a common goal. This is true for archaeology as it is for all research sciences.

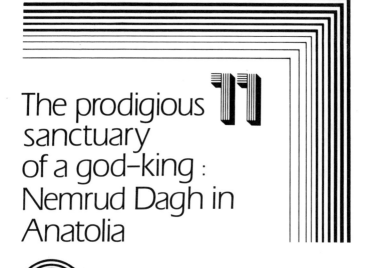

The prodigious sanctuary of a god–king : Nemrud Dagh in Anatolia

emrud Dagh is, indeed, one of the most surprising ancient sites and it was relatively recently discovered. The highest point in the kingdom of Commagene, it is located in Anatolia at the extreme eastern end of Anti-Taurus and to the west of the middle Euphrates. The closest city, though fifty miles to the northwest, is Malatya—Melitene during Greek times—which is in no way attractive for tourists. At the same distance is Samsat, the former Samosate which was the capital of Commagene. Commanding one of the main crossing points on the Euphrates, it grew to be a great city during the Greek and Roman periods, then was taken over by the Francs during the First

Crusade, but today is merely a humble village.

The summit of Nemrud Dagh, listed as having an altitude of 6,050 feet in the official books, is topped by an enormous man-made tumulus, 140 feet high, and surrounded by gigantic statues. It is a prodigious monument, unique in the annals of archaeology, built in the first century of our era by a young king of Commagene, Antiochus, who wanted to be as great as the gods.

Nemrud Dagh means "Nemrod's Mountain". Yes, this is the Nemrod in "Genesis" who "began to be a hero on the earth ..., was a heroic hunter before Jehovah" and built Nineveh and other cities.

There is nothing surprising about the fact that this mountain was named (When? No one knows.) after the fabulous hero who is credited with gigantic works and unmatched accomplishments. It was thought that this character was inspired by the Sumerian god, Nimurta, god of war. In any case, Commagene was quite close to this Mesopotamian and Iranian world where the legend of Nemrod had lost none of its vigor.

A fertile land changed back to steppes

Not so long ago, a visit to Nemrud Dagh represented a small expedition. Approaching it is today made easier by a small road whose construction could be regretted for a variety of reasons, since there are some places which should

Colossal head at Nemrud Dagh. On the second level, the Comagene Tyche, symbol of the ancient prosperity of the region. *Photo by the author*

Nemrud Dagh. In the background, the giant tumulus. In the foreground, huge b
fallen from the giant statues. *Photo by the author*

be approached slowly and wisely. After a long trail a gripping theatrical apparition surges from a lunar landscape, the monstrous cone-shaped tumulus covered with pale stones. When the foot of the tumulus is reached, the giant statues can be perceived which have risen high above for twenty centuries, an impassible guard.

The great Greek geographer, Strabo, who wrote at the beginning of the Christian era, left this note on Commagene, which he may have visited, since he came originally from Cappadoce, in central Anatolia: "It is a small land . . . its size is average, but the soil there is very fertile." One can hardly imagine this ancient image of Commagene when it is seen today with its expanses of ravined, desolate slopes, but the Turkish government is trying to equip the area and bring it back to life. Erosion has reduced this area to steppes though it was once known for its fertility. At the time of the Assyrian Empire they had to give tribute of precious metals, gold and silver, wine, livestock and cedar wood to their powerful neighbors. The cedar was quite simply floated down the Euphrates River. This simple listing shows how rich Commagene was, how much it was envied and how difficult it was for them to retain their independence.

Moreover the region was an important strategic area; it commanded the routes to the middle Euphrates, the passages from Asia Minor to Syria and towards Mesopotamia, used by all the conquerors.

It can seem strange that Nemrud Dagh was "lost" until the middle of the last century. Among the greatest archaeological sites in the East and rich in visible ruins, Palmyra, though in the middle of the Syrian desert, was attentively visited beginning in the eighteenth century; Petra, in Jordan, was explored during the first few years of the 19th century. Leptis Magna, the sumptuous city of Septime Severe, in Libya, was exploited by Louis XIV to supply the columns for Versailles. One hundred years ago, Nemrud Dagh, though crowned with an immense tumulus, and surrounded by titanic statues, remained unknown.

Why should that be surprising? Nemrud Dagh is located in one of the most remote areas of Anatolia, until quite recently devoid of access routes and off the routes on which voyagers of yesteryear could find accommodations. Let us add that, during the time of the Ottoman Empire, foreigners could not very safely travel in Asian Turkey.

Where Lucullus and Mithridates dwelled

The history of Commagene goes back to very ancient times. The name appears for the first time as Kummuhu in the annals of King Salmanasar III of Assyria who reigned in the ninth century B.C. Nothing has ever been found in this country which goes back to this period of Assyrian power.

However, the country certainly had cities, and a capital too. How interesting it would be to find them and know the origins of Commagene which was to become illustrious at the dawn of the Christian era! There are still some great days to come for archaeologists in this country.

In the following centuries, Commagene passed into the hands of the Persians and we will later see what a profound influence Iran had on it. It is naturally included in the conquests of Alexander the Great. When the Conqueror died, it was part of the great Greek state of Seleucides. Taking advantage of the discord which broke up the latter, it became free towards 80 B.C. and had its own kings. Withdrawn in its ring of mountains, naturally well-defended, it could afford to be independent.

It was towards 69 B.C. that Antiochus I took the throne of Commagene. He was an extraordinary sovereign who ruled until 34 B.C., i.e., for about thirty-five years. Historians have devoted him few works, but archaeology is bringing him out of obscurity and learning about him.

With the Romans, Lucullus appeared on the scene in Commagene. It is amusing for us to find him there, the man who was more famous for his dining refinement than for his qualities as a politician or warrior. In fact, he possessed an immense fortune and entertained royally. The famous line of Plutarch goes, "Lucullus is dining at Lucullus' today." By that statement he admonished his cook one day for only having served him a modest meal on the pretext that he was eating alone.

A friend of Cicero and Cato, consul in 74 B.C., Lucullus was responsible for the pursuit of Mithridates. Here is another character of ancient times who is well-known to us, even if it is only through the famous tragedy by Racine. I do not think I would be reproached for devoting a few lines to this prince who is known to History as Mithradites the Great. He was a highlight in one of the darkest pages of Greco-Roman antiquity.

It had been sixty years since Greece had fallen to the power of Rome. It had lost that independence which, despite savage rivalries among cities, had blossomed with splendor. But then Mithridates appeared, the King of Pontus, a civilized barbarian. He raised a revolt in Asia against Rome and massacred all the Italians who lived there. Would Greece free herself from Rome? Sylla, a man of harsh decisions, acted in time. In 87 B.C. he besieged and captured Athens, destroyed everything and massacred the entire population.

After a few sudden actions, Mithridates took refuge in Armenia, whose king was his own son-in-law, with Lucullus in hot pursuit. To reach him the Roman consul had to go through Commagene. It was only with great difficulty that it could have kept itself out of this conflict which raged through all of Asia Minor. It is known that there was then a meeting of Lucullus and Antiochus of Commagene. Did the latter resist? Pliny records that

Samosate was besieged; it is thought that this occurred during this campaign against Mithridates.

From Antony and Cleopatra to the Crusades

Even though it was remote, encircled by mountains and naturally well-defended, Commagene could not escape Rome's grip for long. First, it had to "collaborate" with the Romans. Through the messages of Cicero, it was learned that Antiochus kept the Senate informed of the movements of the Parth troops which instilled such fear in the legions.

The unhappy king knew that his kingdom was coveted because of its strategic position and also for its wealth. Antony, who had been given the responsibility for the Eastern Roman Empire, led a luxurious life with Cleopatra who kept him in constant need of funds. He sent a legate to bring back all the treasures Antiochus possessed. The latter immediately offered a thousand talents. The legate refused this offering and the legions laid siege to Samosate. The campaign was in vain. Even when Antony tried personally, this rival of Augustus, indeed, had to settle not for the thousand talents first offered, but for only 300 generously granted by Antiochus.

A bit later, in 34 B.C., the great king of Commagene died and was buried in the prodigious tomb-sanctuary which he had prepared.

Commagene kept its relative autonomy for a short time thereafter but, after a last hopeless struggle, it was definitively incorporated into the Roman Empire.

After that time it supplied troops for Rome: one mounted squadron and some archers who had a great reputation. The Emperor Vespasian brought the royal family to Rome where it was absorbed by the Roman aristocracy. An inscription was deciphered on a colossus of Memnon about a certain Julia Balbilla who was proud of having been a descendant of the kings of Commagene. She was then accompanying the emperor Hadrian on his visit to Egypt in 130 A.D., a last witness of this dynasty which was so illustrious... But did Julia Balbilla know that one of her ancestors lay on Nemrud Dagh in a tomb of elegant dimensions and surpassing in beauty the Egyptian pyramids?

The Crusaders came to Commagene. It is known that, during the First Crusade, they founded the county of Edessa (Edessa is now the Turkish city, Urfa, less than sixty-three miles from Nemrud Dagh) whose vast seigniory lasted only a short time, fifty years. They made a stronghold of Samosate, the ancient capital of Commagene, and we would like to know if they extended their border to the base of Nemrud Dagh. Blond individuals are found in this area with light eyes and their presence does not go unnoticed. It is said that they are the descendants of Crusaders.

I may have dwelled too long on these pages of

the history of Commagene. They must be kept in mind when this region is visited which has so pathetically changed since ancient times and become one of heavy solitude.

A site lost, then rediscovered

The modern discovery of Nemrud Dagh deserves to be recounted. A young Prussian officer was the first European to visit Nemrud Dagh and describe it. He was on a mission among the Ottoman troops during the war between Turkey and Egypt in 1839. His name was Helmuth von Moltke and he was to have a brilliant career commanding the Prussian army in the Franco-Prussian War.

While traveling through Commagene as a reconnaissance officer, Moltke observed the ancient monuments he found and even made some excellent drawings. Nevertheless, he did not know about the prodigious monument atop Nemrud Dagh though the high terrain often served him as a reference point. At about the same time, an English traveller, Ainsworth, visited Commagene and suggested that Assur—the famous Assyrian capital—could have been located on Nemrud Dagh which, almost unexplored, was steeped in legends.

Fifty years went by. In 1881 a German engineer, Karl Sester, saw the monument of Nemrud Dagh and gave an account in a letter to the Academy in

Berlin. It was at first thought that his description, in which he spoke of giant statues at the summit, was just his imagination . . .

In turn, the Turkish government took an interest in Nemrud Dagh. It appointed Hamdy Bey, director of the Imperial Ottoman Museum in Constantinople, and Osgan Effendi, professor at the School of Fine Arts, to make a survey of it. The two Turkish experts left us an excellent description of their expedition. Though they made their ascent of Nemrud Dagh in May, they were hampered by snow and needed a large team to clear it since, in places, it reached depths of some fifteen feet.

The site was now described, at least super-ficially, but it remained buried in mystery. Another half-century passed. In 1938 a German archaeol-ogist, Professor Friedrich Karl Dörner, accom-panied by his colleague, Rudolf Naumann, arrived at Commagene. Would Nemrud Dagh finally break out of its silence? Nothing of the sort; war broke out. One would almost believe that the sacred mountain was surrounded by genie guards . . .

In 1947 an American, Theresa Goell, took a great interest in reading the ancient reports on Nemrud Dagh and planned an expedition to it. But, at the same time, Friedrich Karl Dörner had decided not to give up the task. It was thus that Nemrud Dagh as well as a site near Arsameia, where the sanctuary of Antiochus' father had been built, were excavated and studied by an American expedition and a German one. One can hardly help admiring the tenacity that these archaeologists must have displayed to take part in such an adventure. Everything was against them: the distance to the nearest city, the well nearest to Nemrud Dagh was three hours away on foot, the extreme heat during the day, no trees, no plants, it was impossible to find shade, the frequent storms, and there were even bears and wolves which roamed in the area.

"I have built this monument in my glory and that of my gods."

Thus the mystery of Nemrud Dagh, summit and supreme sanctuary of Commagene built by King Antiochus, was finally solved. The site yielded a colossal head in his image with youthful features, serene and regular lines, a portrait which bears a great likeness to Alexander the Great. Of all the dynasties which sprang from the conquests of the Babylonian Victor, he seems to us a unique personage with his religious zeal, his conceptions of art and, also, the expression of his pride. For the construction of a divine dwelling-place, a *hiérothésion*, he chose the most spectacular mountain in his kingdom because he was "the closest to the celestial throne of Zeus." A veritable living god, he declared, quite plainly, in one inscription, "I, Antiochus, built this monument in my glory and that of my gods." Actually, he considered himself the equal of the gods and immortal. In sculptures he figures on the same footing with Zeus, Hercules and Apollo.

The story of this sanctuary which, it has been written, is "one of the glories of the Greek world," Antiochus himself had written in "inviolate letters which will last for eternity," on the bases of the gigantic statues which stand on the eastern and western terraces of the sanctuary. It is a long text in which pride is mixed with piety and which is, moreover, a very great piece of ancient literature. I believe it is worthy of a long quotation here:

"I always believed that piety is, of all goods, not only that which is possessed with the most certainty, but also that which is the most sweetly enjoyed by mortals, that it is piety which renders its use enviable, and, during my entire life, I have been observed to respect the gods as the most faithful guardians of my kingdom and as an incomparable pleasure for my heart. This is how I was able to miraculously avoid great dangers, that I was able to easily achieve great accomplishments which afforded little hope, and that I have been granted with a long blissful life.

"Having taken the throne, I made of my kingdom—ruled by a just regime, thanks to my pious sentiments—a haven common to all the gods and, after having adorned their images with all artistic resources as is the ancient custom of the Persians and Greeks, happily my blessed ancestors, I rendered them magnificent honors by celebrating sacrifices and solemn feasts which were due them according to the ancient laws and common traditions among men, or which were instituted by myself.

"It was thus that I conceived the scheme to construct, near the celestial thrones and on a foundation far from the ravages of weather, *hiérothésion* where my body, after being waked amid benedictions, will sleep the eternal sleep, separated from the pious soul which will ascend towards the celestial regions of Jupiter."

Incidentally, these are expressions of a fervor which was very rare in religion at that time. Exegetes can study this text at length and find curious details which mark an unexpected divergence from the usual Greco-Roman mythological rubbish. Of course, some great classical gods still appear, such as Zeus and Apollo, but this is, at the same time, a confusion of several gods and a single mythological abstraction; it is, in a certain way, a precursor of monotheism. Note the pious zeal also, whose very terms, be they sometimes so solemn, are touching because of their profound sincerity. Antiochus saw divine intervention in the affairs of this world and believed in a life hereafter for a soul separated from its body. It could be said that, half a century before Christianity, certain themes seem already to announce its coming.

Here and there on the summit three terraces had been cut out of the rock—to the east, west and north—and it was the stones from these structures which heaped up at the summit formed the tumulus which reached a height of 166 feet.

Antiochus undoubtedly lies under this tumulus. Excavating it is a unique temptation. But how? This artificial hill is formed out of a monstrous heap of stones which slip under the feet when an ascent is attempted. Destroy the tumulus methodically to uncover its secrets? This is an unreasonable dream. Sink a veritable tunnel to reach its heart? This would raise serious difficulties, in particular, by causing a veritable avalanche of stones. After all, isn't it better that Antiochus, the divine king, be granted the tranquility of his last sleep?

The metamorphosis of gods

In front of the eastern terrace a monumental altar was built faced by statues which average thirty feet in height. Most of them are broken-up, fallen over and eaten away. The crackled stone gives the faces the appearance of wrinkles of venerable age. It is like a giants' cemetery in a superhuman setting. In the cortege of the gods is found Antiochus' throne which he had explained in the inscription mentioned above: "I had a statue of myself placed in the middle of those benevolent gods, thus adding new wealth to the majesty of the ancient gods, and because I wanted to represent the constant preoccupation I had vowed to the immortal gods."

What especially holds the attention is that these sculpted gods of Nemrud Dagh are, one might say, hybrids, just like the civilization of the kingdom of Commagene located in the heart of Anatolia which was already a rich civilization and which, essentially Iranian and Greek, strongly reflects the influence of its neighbor, Persia. Also, Antiochus claimed that he was both a descendant of Alexander the Great through his mother, a Seleucidan princess, and of the Persian dynasty through his father, Mithridates Callinicos.

Thus, to represent the sun-god, Apollo is curiously confused with Mithra, the great Iranian divinity whose cult was to penetrate so deeply into the Roman world, even into Gaul, bringing to it a high moral sensibility and the hope of redemption. Zeus is, on his part, confused with Ahura-Mazda, the chief god of the Achemenides. Art at Nemrud Dagh is also a composite. The gods are all represented in the Greek style, but their colossal dimensions are borrowed from Persian art. As for the eagles and lions, they seem to have come from Persepolis.

One is unavoidably struck by the strange beauty of the faces, by their lively expressions and noble serenity. However, the artists concentrated on the faces and strangely neglected the bodies which are stiff supports made of huge blocks, stacked up and badly trimmed. It is not known how the heads came to be separated from the bodies and tumbled down to the foot of the terraces. Earthquake? It has been suggested and, in fact, the region has many seismic tremors. But these heads are, for the most part, in good condition which would not be the case had they been

brutally thrown to the ground. In this regard we
can only guess.

A living sanctuary

The monumental ensemble at Nemrud Dagh
was not a dead sanctuary, withdrawn to the
heights to achieve celestial solitude. On the
contrary, Antiochus, the inscriptions say, wanted
to establish the center of a living cult of his gods
and himself. The texts on the bases of colossal
statues give the details on sumptuous ceremonies
which were to have taken place the tenth and
sixteenth days of each month, the dates of the
anniversary and enthronement. All the rites are
specified; the golden crowns to adorn the heads of
the gods, the offerings of incense and perfumes to
be placed on the altars, and the Persian vestments
for the priests to wear.

The crowds of participants would be treated to
a sumptuous feast. The priest designated for the
divine service receives strict instructions on this
subject: "He will cover the sacred tables with large
platters of food and fill large urns, from those
which are located under the press, with a rich
mixture of wines and will hurry to greet all those
present, those living in the area or foreigners. He
will permit the entire assembly to enjoy the feast.
He will take for himself the part of the offerings
which belong, by custom, to the priest, and
distribute my generous gifts so that they will

partake freely and as they wish, in order that each shall receive all that is due to him and rejoice where he chooses without any reason to make a complaint about the provisioning of the feast."

Even musicians are provided for at the sacred place, and their functions are hereditary as is witnessed by this passage in the inscription, "As for the many musicians I have engaged there myself and those who will later be there engaged, their sons, daughters and descendants, instructed in the same arts, shall be required to perform their functions at the assemblies on the dates set by myself."

Climbing the stony slopes of Nemrud Dagh, one imagines the long processions which ascended the sacred mountain celebrating the power of the gods and the glory of a pious and stately king in this impressive setting which lends itself to raising the spirit and exalting it.

And yet the organization of these feasts leaves one perplexed. We have King Antiochus who decided that they would take place twice a month, in winter as well as summer, and, as we have seen, these were not simple feasts. The faithful were to climb to the summit of Nemrud Dagh in procession; there they were to feast, drink their fill and perform pompous ceremonies. Everything goes as if, expressing his extreme willfulness on this subject, the king of Commagene was not familiar with weather on earth, the burning summers and winter snows. No one who knows Nemrud Dagh could imagine going there to feast during some months of the year, or even lingering there. So, were the instructions of Antiochus intended to forever remain a dead document? This is not possible. In any case, no trace has been found of buildings or accommodations for pilgrims who may have tried to climb Nemrud Dagh during an unfavorable month. A change of climate over the centuries has been suggested, but, without a doubt, it was barely any different two thousand years ago.

The monumental ensemble of Nemrud Dagh, built by Antiochus I, is well-dated by his reign which, as I said, extended from 69 to 34 B.C. Maybe an even more exact date is possible. Indeed, one sculpture found on the eastern terrace, which shows a lion with its body speckled with stars, has been attentively studied. An American expert, Otto Neugebauer, noting the conjunction of the three planets, Jupiter, Mercury and Mars, written in Greek, has established a veritable horoscope corresponding to the month of July in 62 B.C. It may be thought that this is the very date of the foundation of the prodigious sanctuary.

The Hellenistic kingdom of Commagene was singularly shortlived; it hardly lasted a century, but it had created and gave proof of an astonishing civilization amid the mountains. Some scraps of history were all that were known of it, but archaeology is now teaching us how magnificent it was. It is a lost world that has been found again.

Palace of the Thousand and One Nights in the Desert : Okhaydhir

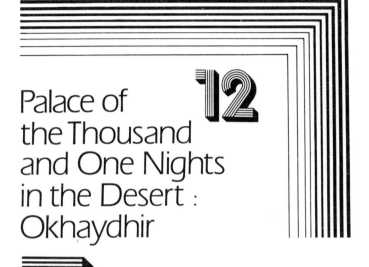

12

There is a vast and eerie castle in the Mesopotamian desert, Okhaydhir, that people interested by military architecture love to visit. Its beauty and the quality of its defenses cannot help but inspire admiration, while its age (we will later see that it was built in the 9th century) shows the extraordinary lead which the East had acquired regarding the construction of fortresses.

Okhaydhir is located about ninety-three miles southwest of Baghdad and slightly west of Babylon. Thirty-seven miles from the Euphrates, it rises from the middle of the desert—a flat desert of unyielding solitude with no settlements, no oases

in this expanse frequented only by a few shepherds and their flocks of sheep.

To reach the lost castle, one must first go to
Kerbela a large and populous city, one of the
sacred cities of the Moslem Chiites. From there
one follows the narrow desert trail for thirty-one
miles, sometimes hindered by the sands.

The desert gives the impression of becoming
heavier and more barren, while Kerbela fades in
the distance as if the castle needed a completely
barren setting to fully set off its qualities.

A long time before it is reached, it appears as a
mass emerging as in a mirage from a limitless
horizon. As it is approached, its contours become
more distinct; its towers and buttresses form huge
streaks of light and shadow. This "Aigues-Mortes"
of the desert, set on perfectly flat ground of tawny
colors, presents a surprising sight. It makes one
think of the first travelers who, not long ago,
approached slowly at their horses' pace. Sometimes it is regretted that transportation is now so
rapid that we almost brutally find ourselves in the
presence of such a monument.

Archaeological pioneers

The first Europeans to reach Okhaydhir
were real explorers. In the 18th century, an
English voyager saw it and noted a brief description. A century and a half had passed before
another European visited it. It was Louis Massi-

gnon, in 1908, who was, as we now know, to become famous as an expert on Islam and the East and teach at the Collège de France. He was only twenty-five when he was put in charge, on behalf of the French Oriental Archaeological Institute, of an expedition to Mesopotamia. He had heard of the castle in the desert and set out to find it. This was no easy task. Having received official recommendations and speaking fluent Arabic he assembled an escort and reached Okhaydhir after a long trip on horseback.

There, things went badly; Massignon was attacked by an armed Arab band. "My escort," he recorded, "knew that they were outnumbered and fled at the first shot. Almost alone, I was subjected to salvos of gunfire from the members of a *Harka* who wanted revenge for a police operation in which several of them had been killed the year before ... The escort rejoined me and we were able to take up positions in the castle. We spent an hour beginning the work of making sketches, taking photos and trying to converse with them. The *Harka's* attitude was hostile so I had to admit that the position was untenable and headed back ... I returned with a large escort ...."

I quoted this passage in order to emphasize that certain archaeological research is by no means restful. Today the only danger one braves, in going to Okhaydhir, is to see one's car buried in sand. Only sixty years ago there was the risk of gunshots and a few other dangers as well. Once back in Baghdad, Louis Massignon had to ter-

minate his expedition when he suffered a serious
malaria attack and, on top of that, an epidemic of
the plague ravaged the city.

A great time for brave pioneers! Later, in 1909,
the dangers notwithstanding, an English woman
arrived at Okhaydhir—Miss Gertrude Lowthian
Bell. Her name remains a legend in the East.

Miss Bell was the daughter of a master black-
smith in Yorkshire. After extensive studies, she
joined her uncle who was at that time a minister
in Teheran. Having learned Persian, Turkish
and Arabic she made several trips in the East
for research and exploration. Enthralled at the
same time by both Islam and Archaeology, she
worked in Syria, Iraq and Anatolia. Five years
after her trip to Okhaydhir she succeeded in
crossing the entire northern part of the Arabian
Peninsula. This was a veritable conquest that
won her a gold medal from the London Geograph-
ical Society.

With the First World War she began a new
career in politics. She was called to Iraq in 1916,
which the English were liberating from the
Turkish-German troops. This was the period of the
"Arab Revolt". She worked closely with Colonel
T.E. Lawrence who was himself originally an
archaeologist.

After the war when the English were granted
the mandate for Iraq, she was awarded the
position of "Eastern Secretary" at Baghdad, which
gave her a sort of omnipotence in Mesopotamian
politics. Nevertheless, she retained her intense

interest in archaeology and founded a museum of Mesopotamian antiquities in Baghdad.

During a visit to Okhaydhir, to which she devoted a great deal of writing, one can hardly restrain from evoking the name of this extraordinary woman. She played an immense role and her personality still remains intriguing. At her death a French archaeologist, who had been among her friends, devoted a few lines to her. "Why did she, from the time of her youth, prefer a wandering solitary life? She never explained this, to my knowledge, not even to her friends. The archaeologist merely glimpses in the light of Corinne's words that, for a woman, the heart has its reasons: the love of science and glory is often just the 'splendid mourning of happiness'."

A catalog of medieval fortifications ahead of its time

A traveller in Iraq, though having seen all the remains of ancient civilizations in Mesopotamia, will always be fascinated by Okhaydhir castle. Many circumstances are united to cause this reaction: the paradox of such a structure in the middle of the desert, the massiveness and discipline of the construction, and also the fact that there are fortresses and defense designs there that date from antiquity, adopted much later in our western castles. We find ourselves trying to make difficult reconciliations and, nevertheless, as I shall later emphasize, Okhaydhir was built in the ninth century and thus predates similar constructions in Europe by three to four centuries.

One of the remarkable things about this castle is that it is of stone, the bricks having merely been used as trim. While travelling through Iraq, after a while you get tired of the brick structures which predominate because of the very nature of the soil. They usually end up quite formless sad ruins, most of the time resembling huge heaps of dried mud. As for Okhaydhir, stone covers it with a golden patina to which it owes the intact condition in which we now admire it.

Nothing is more strict, more subordinated to symmetry than the design of this castle. It is completely enclosed in a square surrounding wall totalling 2640 feet in length, alternately bordered by semi-circular towers and buttresses. There is a large round tower in each corner. A fortified door provides access through the center of each of the four sides. The one in the north wall serves as the main entrance and opens directly onto the extensive structures which form the residential palace inside. A tour must first be made of the exterior of this immense wall whose entire length is so well preserved that it gives an impressive, powerful appearance. The presence of a classical defense is first noted in the vertical battlements on the huge buttressed arches matched by semi-circular towers, and above, a line of holes for archers.

Then, by climbing one of the four interior stairs

located in the corners of the walls, the top of the fortification can be inspected, not by the passage with its battlements extending the length of the wall which has now disappeared, but through a corridor which runs directly below it and con- stitutes a basic part of its defenses. In the past it was vaulted, eight feet wide, and enclosed within the thickness of the wall throughout its entire length. This "shaft" (this is the exact term) had numerous holes for archers which enabled them to shoot not only towards the outside, but also into the interior court in case the invader penetrated.

Such an arrangement (ingenious since it protected the defenders while allowing them to quickly move to exposed points) was later used rarely in Europe. Only one castle in France has one, that of Coudray-Salbart, near Niort, one of the largest fortified castles of our Middle Ages and unfortunately too little known.

Vertical battlement, archer holes, shaft, etc. . . . an entire catalog of good medieval fortifications was already displayed at Okhaydhir in the 9th century A.D. i.e., several centuries ahead of Western castles. This is a fact which should be repeatedly pointed out and emphasized.

An immense, sumptuous palace

Through the door in the center of the northern wall, which acted as the entrance of honor, one penetrates into the interior of the enceinte. First a vast hall of a monumental appearance, divided into three naves by massive columns that support powerful arcades, is entered. The mosque is located on the right as one enters, and is made up of a court bordered by a porch of which remains only a few fragments of columns.

The residential palace rises in the center of the immense rectangle of the walls. It, too, is a rectangular structure of gigantic dimensions: almost 300 feet long by 250 feet wide. Thick walls edged with huge circular buttresses completely surround it. Thus, an attacker who had penetrated into the court would then encounter this second line of defense.

The entire interior castle, which is actually an immense palace, is merely composed of a ground floor and terrace above. The design is simple, majestically placed around a rectangular central court, 107 by 88 feet; nevertheless, you lose your way walking through courts, rooms and corridors bathed in a pleasant semidarkness essential for withstanding temperatures which in the hot season are among the world's highest.

These vast chambers can be imagined, in semi-obscurity, as decorated with stucco, finely carved wood, rich carpets and silks. All the pomp of the East was displayed here, surrounded by servants and slaves as well as soldiers who stood guard on the ramparts. Today, however, the setting has been stripped, the people are gone and you are alone in a castle wrapped in silence.

We will probably never know what great

personalities built and inhabited this Versailles of the desert where not only luxury but also life was a paradox. I suppose that the surroundings were not more fertile in ancient times than now, and that most supplies had to be brought from the banks of the Euphrates. Let us not forget that a good share of the tales of the Thousand and One Nights originated in Baghdad which is not far away. How could they not have come from a land of mirages where a castle such as that of Okhaydhir belonging to an unreal world where challenges and fairy tales were united?

Trying to determine the construction date

What did such a castle represent and when was it built? As one might expect, this question is important and has caused some debate, in particular, between Okhaydhir's two "discoverers," Louis Massignon and Gertrude Bell.

The former, while complaining of the lack of inscriptions that could have determined the date, estimated that it had been built between the 4th and 7th centuries A.D. As for Gertrude Bell, she believes there were some Greek influences in the castle's architecture. In a word, Okhaydhir was thought to be extremely old. Since then, however, it has been considerably rejuvenated. The Iraqi archaeological services have taken a great interest in this prodigious monument and done some excavations and restorations. They discovered

that one of the rooms of the palace had originally
been a mosque. It must be admitted that Okhaydhir is earlier than Islam. The date can even be
specified as between 820 and 860 A.D.

A good hypothesis is that the fortified palace
was constructed by Ibn Moussa, nephew of the
Caliph, El Mansour, founder of Baghdad, after he
himself was persuaded to renounce his position as
Caliph. The palace of the Thousand and One
Nights, Okhaydir could also have been a kind of
gilded prison for a forced retirement.

However, this single hypothesis is not sufficient to explain the castle's enormous defenses.
These emphasize that the desert has always been
a worrisome subject for the powers established in
the Mesopotamian plains. Okhaydhir represented
a mighty fortress for surveillance and emprison-
ment thirty-two miles from the Euphrates River.

In front of the north façade of the castle, that of
the main entrance, you will see a vast building
which extends alongside it, but which is unfortunately very dilapidated. This was a set of
annexes to the castle which must have been
barracks, caravansaries and stables. A large
garrison was required to man Okhaydhir. There
was a problem getting water but it had been
solved with a network of underground canals
and reservoirs (very similar to the *foggaras* in
the Sahara) the remains of which are still visible.

Eastern supremacy in military architecture

But we must reconsider the construction date, the 9th century. As western people, we would tend to attribute such a monument, because of its defensive system, to the 11th or 13th centuries. Otherwise how can such advances in military architecture in the East be explained? At the time Okhaydhir was built, this land had inherited the defensive systems of the Assyrians, later, of the Parths and Sassanids, and, above all, those of Rome, retained by the Byzantines, which were passed on in turn by the Armenians. Among the assets of these systems was, for example, the awesome surrounding wall featuring all the defensive improvements which, precisely in the ninth century, were built to protect Ani, the Armenian capital at that time in northeast Anatolia along what is now the Turkish-Russian border.

There is no study more thrilling than that of military architecture throughout the East. It is certainly complex and of unbounded proportions. The respective contributions of the civilizations that have developed between the Mediterranean and Iran must be revealed. Only concerning Okhaydhir we remain confused. As I mentioned, Gertrude Bell saw Greek influences while Louis Massignon emphasized Sassanid traits.

In any case, the Iraqi castle cannot be attributed to Arabian architects. Byzantine architects serving the caliphs may be considered. Recent excavations have provided some fragments on just this subject, notably the bases of columns which indeed seem to be Byzantine. A conclusion cannot be made at the present stage of study on the castle. It is troubling that its parentage is so doubtful, and that it will probably remain forever an orphan. Just the same it would be interesting to know who was the inspired master (or at least where he came from) who had such a splendid, original and defensively perfect edifice erected in the desert.

A sensational discovery in the heart of a Mayan pyramid : Palenque, the man-god

Among the great devastated remains of the Mayan civilization of which southern Mexico is proud, some are famous and attract a throng of visitors each year. Such is the case for Uxmal or Chichén Itzá, in Yucatán, which appears in the international tourist *gotha* (guide). Their main monuments are almost all cleared and the wounds of time have been bandaged. They can be reached by good paved routes in air-conditioned busses from Cook Travel. In the evening, luxurious hotels welcome the exhausted tourists after they have climbed the stairs of the pyramids.

But there are other Mayan cities which remain not so accessible, protected by thick walls of vegetation or by their remoteness which reserve the joys of solitary contemplation for the traveller. This is the case of Palenque, precisely where Mayan art undoubtedly reached its highest peaks.

The illustrious city is located in the state of Chiapas near the state of Tabasco. It is backed by a spur of the great Chiapas mountain range which borders on Guatemala. Before it is a huge green expanse of plains which extend to the Gulf of Mexico about 208 miles away.

Nothing could be more tropical than the immense forest in which Palenque firmly sits hidden in a veritable bedrock of vegetation. The trees reach a height of 100 to 130 feet. Marvelous species fill this opulent forest such as the American mahogany and red cedar, both prized for their wood, and the sapodilla whose sap is gathered to make chewing gum.

This profuse and almost menacing vegetation makes for a heavy atmosphere which seems to wage an unceasing war against the men who would want to strangle it by timbering. The climate, oppressive and stifling, also makes it heavy with the air saturated with water vapor. Though forbidding for man, it vibrates with the presence of fauna: birds of shimmering colors, parrots, wild turkeys, toucans and red-throated trogons. Sometimes the branches rustle from the monkeys while jaguars leap through the underbrush where reptiles abound.

A site forbidden by nature

For a long time Palenque was protected by nature itself which covered it before finally devouring it whole. Nevertheless, it was known as early as the eighteenth century. In 1785 official expeditions visited the site and sent back illustrated reports to Charles III, King of Spain.

At the beginning of the last century a curious voyager appeared on the scene at Palenque and became a character in its story. He was named, or at least called himself, Baron Jean-Frederic-Maximilian de Waldeck. He was a peculiar man, an adventurer throughout his life (we will later see to what a ripe old age he lived), an impostor at his fancy. He was born in Vienna in 1766; at nineteen, he was at the Cape of Good Hope; upon his return, he went to Paris, became a naturalized French citizen, took part in the siege of Toulon with Napoleon and followed the French troops to Egypt. Maybe, when he later approached the Mayan pyramids, he could again hear an echo of the famous sentence about the contemplation of centuries... After the capitulation, to escape the English, he fled to Eastern Africa, boarded one of Surcouf's ships and travelled to the Indian Ocean. Later he took part in the liberation of Chile then went to Guatemala and Mexico.

"At the age at which most archaeologists go into retirement," humorously notes Sir Eric Thompson, a great Mayanist, "Waldeck began his work at seventy in the Mayan region and confounded all the opinions on the unhealthfulness of the Central American forests by living to a hundred and nine." Yes, this extraordinary character, born during the reign of Louis XV, died during the Third Republic ... When he returned from America he devoted himself to painting and engraving for which he had some talent. He had his first two paintings exhibited at the Paris Show at the age of a hundred and one and exhibited various paintings in the years that followed. He died from an accident in the street and it was indeed his own fault. He had unwisely turned his head to ogle a pretty girl. At his age ...

He stayed at Palenque for two years making diagrams and drawings, and published, in 1837, *An Archaeological and Picturesque Trip Through Yucatán*. It's a pity he cared not the least bit about authenticity. His sketches are, from this point of view, similar to the title of "Baron" he gave himself. He produced oddly inaccurate images of Mexican architecture and sculpture which suffered, alas, immensely ...

Archaeologists begin their work

Many years later ... Palenque slumbered in the forest waiting to reveal its secrets. One may be astonished that systematic research was begun only forty years ago. But think of the enormous tasks Mexican specialists have to perform! At this time they have catalogued more than eleven

Nemrud Dagh. Head of Apollo. The person in the photo gives an idea of its size.
Photo by the author

View of the exterior fortification of Okhaydhir castle showing one of the four d which rise up in the center of each side. *Photo by the author*

thousand sites for pre-Hispanic civilizations. Their exploration, for the most part, requires enormous efforts. In Mexico, archaeologists mostly work far from inhabited areas. They have to clear the areas before beginning archaeological work. Once the monuments have been cleared, they have to restore and take all necessary steps to protect them from constant natural invasion. Let us add, and this is perhaps the number one problem, that the remains of pre-Columbian civilizations are usually made up of ensembles of considerable size where temples and palaces have accumulated. Let Palenque be an example for comparison; we can only fix its boundaries with great difficulty. Besides the immense area which is now cleared, the city extended over a length of at least five miles east to west.

It was in 1949 that the exploration of Palenque was entrusted to a brilliant specialist, Alberto Ruz Lhuillier. Thanks to his perfect knowledge of Mayan civilization and architecture, and also his intuition and perseverance, in 1952 he was to write one of the most sensational discoveries ever recorded into the annals of archaeology.

Born in 1906 in Paris of a Cuban father and French mother, Alberto Ruz Lhuillier has been a naturalized Mexican since 1940. He first studied in Paris, then in Mexico. From his very first contact with Mexico he was irresistibly attracted by pre-Columbian civilizations. His calling became clear; he obtained degrees in archaeology and returned to Paris to study for short periods. In 1938 he began his career in excavations. He quickly became one of the greatest experts in pre-Columbian civilizations and, in 1949, was appointed director of research in the Mayan area. It was in this capacity that he took interest in the Palenque site. He was forty-three at that time.

The mysterious stairway

The Palenque archaeological zone extends over natural terraces which suggest a giant stairway. From the dense vegetation emerge the prodigious structures which are among the most perfect of the Mayan civilization. First there is the "palace" which displays a collection of patios, galleries and chambers, spread over an elevated platform, over 290 feet long by almost 230 feet wide. Secondly, there are a whole series of temples, architectural jewels set on high pyramids. Modern men have given them names: the North Temple, the Count's Temple, the Cross Temple, the Temple of the Sun, the Lion Temple, the Temple of the Foliated Cross, and the Temple of Inscriptions. What an ensemble, both powerful and well-proportioned! The structures vie with the tropical trees in height as if to affirm the power of man motivated by supernatural zeal against nature. The sculptures mark the white stone with delicate seals. That a people could construct such architecture eloquently proves not only its spiritual zeal but also its social development. The group of human beings who lived there attained a high degree of organization which was brought forth by an irresistible compulsion to satisfy their mysticism.

What also can be said for this people who did not have the wheel to enable them to easily transport materials or even iron tools to work with? More prosaically it must be recognized that Palenque had, during its golden age, considerable resources. The great forest supplied wood, while the adjacent plain, cut by several meandering rivers and lakes, allowed prolific irrigated cultivation. The many animals that inhabited the area, and fish which teemed in the waters, provided on their side abundant food.

Palenque was, at the same time, a political power, holy site, city of art and scientific center. It was also the burial site for great personalities. The discovery of Ruz Lhuillier was to prove this.

The Temple of Inscriptions, next to the "palace", was the scene of this discovery. It has this name, and also that of the Temple of Law, because of three stone panels bearing hieroglyphic inscriptions, one of the longest known Mayan texts. The building is located on a high pyramid with a rectangular base and is reached by a steep stairway. Five doors, with pillars bearing beautiful reliefs, open through the facade.

A huge slab of stone had already been noted in the floor of the temple which had twelve holes cut through. These were blocked by stone plugs, perfectly fitted, which provided a hermetic seal. Ruz Lhuillier thought that there must have been a

structure beneath the temple. He wanted to find
out for sure. During excavation, steps of a stairway
leading to the heart of the pyramid were uncovered. An incredible discovery! In fact, none of
the many pyramids built by the ancient Americans
had this kind of arrangement.

This happened in 1949. The steep stairway had
been filled long ago by earth and stones, and
removing this rubble pail by pail was a tedious and
difficult job to which Ruz Lhuillier devoted no less
than four separate excavations. In 1949 he had
cleared twenty-three steps and again that many in
1950 and had reached a depth of forty-nine feet
from the summit of the pyramid. In 1951 he cleared two small ventilation tunnels which extended
out horizontally to the west side. At this point the
stairway changed direction. Until then, it descended to the east; the second flight headed west.

What was this stairway—the first discovered
within the heart of a pre-Columbian pyramids—
and where did it lead? The question remained
unanswered after three years of work. Anxiety
increased as the excavation reached greater
depths and, simultaneously, more problems were
encountered. The rubble was more firmly packed
down, and it could be observed that the stones had
been sealed by calcareous deposits formed over
the centuries. Work had to be done in the heavy,
humid and dusty air, in cramped spaces where
movement was difficult, amid the discouraging
impression that the removal of small shovelfuls
of rubble would continue endlessly.

Six young people sacrificed

The fourth excavation began in 1952. Thirteen
more steps were cleared. The stairway came to an
end, then a corridor began. It was located at a
depth of about sixty-five feet below the temple
floor. The goal was in sight... Ruz Lhuillier was
convinced of this, but he had not yet reached the
end of his problems. He attacked a wall made of
stone and limestone mortar which formed a
compact mass that proved to be over nine feet
thick.

Once the wall was destroyed, a sort of
sepulcher appeared. There were human remains.
The skeletons were tangled, since the bodies had
been literally crushed to be put into such a small
space. The bones were very badly preserved
because of the humidity and calcareous salts
which covered them. It could nevertheless be
determined that six young people, one a woman,
had been buried in this spot. No offering nor object
was found with them.

This discovery was oddly moving. These
people, whose packed remains had been found,
had been sacrificed. Then the intense recollections
of the human sacrifices of the ancient Mexicans
came to mind, especially those of the Aztecs "who
wallowed in blood" and also of the Maya. In the
sacred "cenote" of Chichén Itzá a great number of
bones of men, women and children had been
found. Mayan art complacently shows scenes of
sacrifices haughtily ordered by the gods. Nor-

mally, the heart of the victim was ripped out, but they were also attached to posts and killed with arrows. It also happened that they were thrown from the tops of pyramids. Pitiful offerings to bloodthirsty gods! How had the young men and woman of Palenque been immolated? Was the woman the wife of a dead man? We do not know. The cruel rituals of a civilization, though it was so developed in many ways, appear at the heart of the pyramid. It led to anticipation that, further on, a sacred keep was to be discovered.

"A ghostly chamber, like a palace of ice"

Ruz Lhuillier now found himself in front of an enormous monolithic stone which was set in vertically and had the form of a triangular opening. He examined the setting which was perfectly joined all around. However, on the lower left-hand side he found a small opening which long ago had been plugged up with stones and mortar. A worker probed it, and his mining bar passed through the opening. The stones were pulled out. Ruz Lhuillier pointed an electric light through the part that had been cleared. Behind the heavy monolithic stone he saw a large crypt with bas-reliefs on the walls, and, in the center, an imposing sculpted monument. It seemed a ghostly chamber, shining like a palace of ice.

A moving instant for all of us! Here I must let Ruz Lhuillier tell the story. "From the dark shadow," he wrote, "burst a vision from a fairy tale, a phantasmagorical spectacle, ethereal and not of this world. It was like a vast magic cave sculptured of ice with the walls sparkling and twinkling like snowflakes. Delicate stalactite festoons hung like drapery cords and the stalagmites on the floor resembled the drippings of giant church candles.

"In fact, it gave the impression of an abandoned chapel. Stucco bas-relief figures lined the walls. My eyes fell next to the floor. It was almost entirely covered by a huge slab of sculpted stone in perfect condition.

"While gazing with respect and astonishment, I described the marvelous spectacle to my colleagues but they refused to believe me until I moved away and they could see the fascinating vision with their own eyes. Our eyes were the first to behold it for more than a thousand years..." How much the discovery of the secret chamber of Palenque suggested that of the tomb of Tutankhamen!

The crypt was opened at 1 p.m. on Sunday, June 15, 1952. Many inhabitants of the nearby village had run there and squeezed into the narrow corridor. The stone wedges which ensured the huge monolith's seal with the surfaces were removed. A rope was inserted and the enormous stone was finally turned on its base and pushed over. A narrow passage was thus formed which allowed a person to slide through sideways.

The crypt, into which four steps descend, is not

large. It is made up of a kind of nave, rectangular with four built-in alcoves which face each other. It measures twenty-nine and a half feet long by twelve feet at its widest point. The vault, cut in a triangle, reaches twenty-one and a half feet. Five large stone slabs, blackish with yellow veins, reinforce it. The floor which, when it was discovered, was covered by a calcareous coating from water seepage, is formed of well cut and perfectly joined stone slabs. The walls and vault are made of remarkably cut, polished and dressed stones. The construction is obviously perfect and of a peerless refinement. It has been established that the floor of this crypt is seventy-eight feet below the base of the temple and about six feet below the bottom of the pyramid which constitutes its giant base.

The mystical decor of the Maya

The stucco bas-reliefs that decorate the walls of the crypt and which appeared in the fairy-like deposits which covered them, represent personnages a little larger than life-size. They total nine, the Lords of the Night who reigned over the Mayan subterranean world, and glitter with somptuous ornaments, headdresses with large plumes, their bird helmets, feather cloaks and numerous jewels.

Scattered about in the room are various offerings which I will not try to describe here in detail. Most were placed on the sculptured mon-

The sepulcher at the very bottom of the temple at Palenque. The slab covers the tomb. *Photo Taller*

Made of about two hundred pieces of jade, seashell for the eyes and obsidian
the irises. This is the mask from a corpse at Palenque. *Saint-Clair*

ument in the center. Indeed, the largest of the articles recovered were two heads modeled of stucco. The most beautiful was popularized as the "Palenque Head". Measuring seventeen inches long, it represents a young man whose head has been subjected to the classic artificial cranial deformation of which the Maya were fond, with a bent nose and a receding forehead following the same curve as the nose. The thick hair is held by a headband decorated with water lily flowers just beginning to open up, coming around in front in a kind of crest.

What elegant composition! What a perfect model! The rich decoration that crowns the head does not render the face heavy. The simple, sober features, the wide-open immobile eyes, the slightly contorted mouth, everything contributes to an undoubtedly striking realism but spiritualized by an undefinable quality of nobility and detachment.

But it is about time that I talk about the large monument which occupied almost the entire crypt and around which it was visibly constructed. It looks like a huge block of monolithic stone, roughly cubical, set on a foundation of six decorated supports. The dimensions? Ten feet long, seven feet wide and thirty-nine to forty-three inches high. Its weight has been calculated to be twenty tons.

A finely sculpted slab covers it and juts out over the edges like a cope of great price. It seems the sculptor wanted to fully convey not only the virtuosity of Mayan decorations, but also their mysticism, both of them profuse and complex.

The edges of the stone are adorned with fifty-four hieroglyphs of which a certain number mention data concerning the calendar. A very precious item of information has been deduced from this, the approximate date of 700 A.D.

When the crypt was opened, Ruz Lhuillier and his colleagues assumed the great central monument to be an "altar". The end of the exploration had to be awaited before its function could definitely be stated. However, it could be taken for granted that they stood before the most sacred sanctuary of the city of Palenque. There in the dark depths, the secret rites of the high caste of priests had occurred in which human sacrifices would have had their place.

Ruz Lhuillier was sorely tempted to lift off the great slab cover but this would have been a useless risk if the monolithic stone it covered were solid. Thus probes were first performed through the block directed obliquely towards the center. The first was pushed to seventy inches but still worked against compact stone. To be absolutely sure a second one was performed in the opposite direction. At a bit more than thirty-nine inches a cavity was hit. A wire was inserted through the small hole. It continued a long way and, when it was pulled out, it carried bits of paint. The hole was therefore enlarged and an electric light showed a surface covered with red paint.

The emotion which gripped the team of

excavators is understandable. The enormous monolith was indeed hollow. But what did it contain? No, there could be no hesitation; the sculptured slab had to be removed. But what problems they foresaw! The crypt was so tiny that movement was difficult. The number of workers employed at one time was limited, and the weight to be moved under adverse circumstances approached five tons. The slighest error threatened the magnificent sculptures.

A skeleton lay amid extraordinary jewels

At six o'clock on November 27, 1952, the operation was begun. It would last until the same time the next morning, without interruption for rest or the slightest delay.

It was decided to use simple equipment (on the other hand, what other means could be provided?), basically automobile jacks placed at the angles of the enormous stone slab which weighed, as I said, about five tons.

First a large tree had to be felled, *bari,* a species of mahogany, and cut into pieces of various thicknesses and lengths. Some of these boards would support the jacks and heighten them; others would be inserted under the slab as it was raised; some more would serve as braces to keep the stone from sliding. All these planks had to be brought down the narrow staircase, which was no easy job.

So began the operation of lifting the slab. What strenuous, patient efforts! The slightest error of movement, the collapse of a jack, could have caused this admirable panel of Mayan sculpture to be broken. Ruz Lhuillier and his team worked under extreme tension and wearisome conditions because of the tiny, badly ventilated crypt. The scene was lit by hand-lanterns, and the operation took place in a laborious atmosphere of heavy clamminess.

It took four hours of effort to lift the slab sixteen inches. As soon as the operation was begun, Ruz Lhuillier had observed a deception. He thought that the cavity covered by the slab would be open. No, it was hermetically sealed by a stone lid with a curved shape, perfectly fitted into the solid stone. Fortunately it was provided with holes through which ropes could be passed. In turn, it too was lifted.

Fatigue and emotion overcame Ruz Lhuillier and his team; they were experiencing one of the great moments of archaeology, that science that everyone considers dull but which suddenly, lifting the shroud in which pages of history have been buried, can present you with such moving realities.

What a vision! The cavity was indeed a tomb. A skeleton lay there amid extraordinary jewels. At first sight the sepulcher appeared to have been cut especially for the body it was to receive, tailored, one might say. Its dimensions were, in fact, slightly bigger than those of the skeleton.

The corpse rested on its back, the arms outstretched. All the parts of the skeleton were in place and, though very crumbly, they could be studied. The man, quite stout, was between forty and fifty. His height? It is estimated at five-foot-nine.

A mask made of two hundred pieces of jade

The body had been buried in very rich clothing which, after so many centuries, were merely dust and pigment of the red paint that had colored them. The body must have been wrapped in a shroud, fastened undoubtedly with bone needles of which three have been found, at the throat and shoulders.

Though the fabrics did not resist, all the ornaments and jewels—almost all of jade—have been recovered, and how sumptuous they are, and what variety!

The most sensational piece is indeed the mask, composed of an extraordinary mosaic of jade, two hundred pieces in all. The eyes were of seashell with obsidian irises. To complete the realism, the pupil was represented by a black spot.

When the tomb was opened all these fragments lay around the head. How were they assembled and held together? The remains of a stucco frame were found which, in all probability had been adapted to the face of the deceased and had been later broken. Thanks to a minute

examination of each of the pieces, Alberto Garcia
Maldonado, by trade an engraver, was able to
rebuild the mask which measures nine and two-
thirds inches long by seven and two-thirds inches
across. It is an admirable piece, one of the most
extraordinary works of Mayan art! It can be
admitted that, moulded to the face, it fit the
features exactly and, at this point, represents a
sort of portrait.

But the deceased's head was not adorned with
this mask alone; it was crowned with a coronet.
Forty-one discs, of various shapes and sizes, have
been found which composed it. A jade pendant of
an intense green was found in the debris of the
cranial cavity representing a bat (the Mayan *zotz*),
and was undoubtedly a part of the coronet. There
were ornaments on the ears, in particular, two jade
plates with hieroglyphic inscriptions. The locks of
hair were inserted into jade heads. A mouth
decoration was also found which was maybe
stuck to the mask; it was rectangular and made of
little plates of pyrite with, at each corner, a seashell
disc. A similar ornament appears around the
mouth on the personages who figure in the stucco
bas-reliefs which decorate the crypt walls.

Such were the strange and magnificent ornaments that adorned the head of the illustrious
deceased of Palenque (and I still have not finished
listing all the pieces), but the whole body was
decorated in the same manner: At the neck there
was a necklace of a hundred and eighteen jade
beads; on the chest there was a breastplate of

beads strung on nine concentric threads. Around each arm there was a bracelet of two hundred beads; on each finger, a ring, also jade. On the feet there were large jade pearls and a small man-like idol with the features of the sun-god. Another human figurine was found at the crotch, it was probably sewn to the codpiece.

The brutal fall of a civilization

One question I have not yet brought up is that of the date of the Palenque monument. It can be placed at the end of the seventh or beginning of the eighth century, i.e., around 700 A.D. That was the great era of the Mayan lowlands, that of the flowering of its civilization, arts and sciences. In France this would correspond to the Merovingians, soon to be succeeded by the Carolingians. While in the West the Roman civilization had crumbled and no other had as yet taken its place, in the land of Mexico other admirable civilizations were blossoming and Palenque is one of their highest points. The last date determined for the city is 784 A.D. The Mayan glory then began to fade. A hundred years after the burial of the man-god, it suddenly darkened.

What was the reason for this sudden fall, for this unavoidable death which fell upon such a glittering civilization?

Many hairs have been split on this subject. It has been suggested that Mayan agricultural methods were so primitive and so inefficient (the plow and even the spade were unknown) that, since they were faced with increasing population and danger of famine, a massive emigration took place. The abandon of the great centers has also been thought to have been caused by yellow fever or malaria but it has been demonstrated that these diseases were introduced by the Spanish conquerors.

Sir Eric Thompson, the great Mayanist, has advanced the hypothesis of serious social problems. That the castes of priests and nobles made ever increasing demands and required constantly increasing manpower. One day, the peasants, tired of this band of veritable parasites who produced nothing and weary of working for them, revolted. Violent uprisings broke out chasing or massacring the ruling class, and bringing the peasant leaders to power. Then, the monuments no longer tended, fell into ruin and the vegetation completed their destruction.

This is certainly an attractive hypothesis but it can only be accepted prudently. Nevertheless, concerning this revolt of oppressed men, we would like to have some assurance that it indeed broke out one day. It would satisfy our modern pretentions to justice and liberty. These monuments at Palenque and other great Mayan cities fill us with admiration but also cause a certain uneasiness. We can hardly avoid considering the ruthless demands of the caste that desired them and the oppression of the men who built them.

The discovery of Ruz Lhuillier brought up so many problems! One point at least has been established. First the sepulcher was built, then the crypt and pyramid, space for the stairway having been left inside. In fact, it would have been impossible to insert the monolithic blocks of which the sepulcher is built afterwards. (The sculpted slab alone measures seven square yards and weighs, as I said, five tons). Were the tomb and the giant monument that crowns it prepared while the glorious occupant was alive? This is not known. In any case, after the funeral, the persons whose remains were found at the foot of the heavy stone which forms the crypt were sacrificed. Finally, the stairway was methodically filled so that no one would ever enter the sacred place. Without a doubt, the deceased was considered equal to a god, and his tomb's hermetic seal was to prevent any human power from disturbing his eternal sleep.

Therefore, this pyramid was basically a funeral monument, and this discovery was sensational. Generally it was considered that the pyramids that are scattered throughout Central America were built to serve as massive bases for the temples. In fact this was indeed their original purpose as can be seen throughout the land of the Aztecs as well as that of the Maya. The case of the pyramid of Palenque, built as a sepulcher is the only one known at this time.

The inordinate effort of a whole nation

As soon as the news of this discovery had spread, commentaries were produced on the problem of pyramids in general. Certain ones compared the Mayan pyramids with those of Egypt, wanting to find similarities. Didn't they realize the thousands of years that separate the constructions of the Pharaohs from those of the Maya? And where did they find witnesses of the intermediate steps, the marks of a progression? Others described in a more precise manner the pyramids of Southeast Asia, those of the Khmer country. They rested on a theory according to which America was peopled by immigrants who came from Asia across the Bering Strait. But, here again, no respect at all was paid to chronology for the American pyramids were built before the Asian ones.

There remains an impressive parallel which can be drawn between the ancient Americans and the Egyptians. It is true that, thousands of miles away from one another, two nations who did not know of one another built structures, incredibly huge ones, in the same spirit, that they must have faced the same fearsome problems and that they both solved them with equal mastery in spite of limited technical resources. How much effort, and sacrifice too, was needed to build such pyramids, to extract, transport and cut the stones that were amassed there, and to carve the sculptures! And, as I said, the Maya were able to accomplish such feats while ignorant of the use of the wheel and iron tools.

And, also, such operations were not a simple matter of labour. They required a world of engineers, architects and artists. And what is more, the Maya had to have a rich and evolved economy so that the producing class, the farmers, could not only provide for itself but also underwrite the needs of the throng of builders, added to those of the parasitic castes: the priests and warriors. In Mexico as in Egypt, human masses, for centuries, were able to dedicate themselves completely to inordinate construction. This supposes that all resources were strained to produce these edifices.

Such works throw a cruel light on the organization of Mayan society: a coherent mass, with a hierarchy, obeying its rulers without question, participating in the same savage religious fervor. A king-priest, like the one who was buried in the pyramid at Palenque, was of divine essence. Men were sacrified to surround him with greater honors, to build an indestructible tomb for him. The entire Mayan people, entirely motivated by this mysticism, wanted to participate by its efforts in the benefits the priest-god could dispense in the world beyond.

The construction technique in the stairway and crypt at Palenque shows a perfection which undoubtedly has no equivalent in other ancient American monuments. And, in the crypt, all the works, the stuccoes on the walls, the sculptures on the tomb and the offerings, are masterpieces. What is striking is that they were not made to be seen at all. Just finished, they were buried; then, an enormous pyramid was built on top of them. Indeed, there was the narrow staircase which descended through the solid mass, but this was surely built only for the initiated; it was carefully blocked so that no other person would ever approach the august corpse, and its sumptuous tomb. This is an admirable concept of Mayan art which, consecrated to the gods, scorned human contemplation!

Today, for hurried visitors, the Mexican archaeological services have reconstructed, in the praiseworthy museum at Mexico City, the tomb of Palenque. The jade mask is there as well as the two stucco heads found beside the sarcophagus. However, there is nothing like a visit to Palenque and the sight of the Temple of the Inscriptions in the oppressing tropical forest. Nothing could replace descending these narrow, steep, poorly lit stairs to the bottom where the incomparable funeral chamber opens up. By lingering a bit in this mysterious world, with its sumptuous decorations that reach the heights of perfection, you feel that you take part in this eternal peace sought by the man-god twelve centuries ago.

Printed in Switzerland
Published by Ferni
Distributed by Friends of History